Soulish Leadership

Whose Kingdom Are You Building?

Bert M. Farias

Foreword by Dr. Michael L. Brown

Treasure House

An Imprint of
Destiny Image® Publishers, Inc.
P.O. Box 310
Shippensburg, PA 17257-0310

"For where your treasure is,
there will your heart be also." Matthew 6:21

ISBN 1-56043-329-9

For Worldwide Distribution
Printed in the U.S.A.

This book and all other Destiny Image, Revival Press,
and Treasure House books are available
at Christian bookstores and distributors worldwide.

For a U.S. bookstore nearest you, call **1-800-722-6774**.
For more information on foreign distributors, call **717-532-3040**.
Or reach us on the Internet: **http://www.reapernet.com**

Acknowledgments

Many thanks to all those who supported this project with their labors, prayer, and financial support. Special appreciation goes to my friend, Dr. Michael L. Brown, for writing the Foreword and for his many helpful insights and corrections. Thanks for encouraging me with this first book and for wanting to make it a part of the Brownsville Revival School of Ministry.

Thanks also to my sweet wife, Carolyn, and our precious son, Daniel, for providing me with the constant hope and inspiration that I need to be a man of God. I love you so much.

Loving gratitude also to my parents, John and Maria Farias, who have always loved me and been there for me. I love you more than you will ever know.

Finally, and most importantly, to my heavenly Father, my Lord Jesus Christ, and the mighty Holy Spirit for the love, guidance, and favor to complete this project. It's only with Kingdom purposes in mind that I can even willingly and with a pure conscience submit such a book. May Your Kingdom and Your holiness be established in the hearts of Your leaders and people everywhere.

Contents

Preface

A small part of the message in this book was first preached at a conference in 1995. Upon hearing it, three highly respected ministers suggested that it be put into book form. Once the two-hour taped message was transcribed and placed in my hands, I began to realize that there was much more in my spirit concerning this word. In 1997 I began to seriously write the remainder of the book, and now here is the finished version.

I believe one of the key characteristics of the revival spirit is when leaders with no hidden agendas begin to gather together. This book is about having pure motives and no hidden agendas. It is about building the Kingdom of God, as opposed to building your own. It's a book that was born as a burden in my heart when I served for nine years on the mission field and witnessed firsthand the incredible amount of jealousy, competition, and selfish ambition that exists among ministers. It was also born out of a heartfelt desire to see a greater citywide spirit of unity and revival prevail among ministers and churches.

This book was also born out of my own personal struggles as a young minister. You see, the ministry is an idol to many. We are often taught the how-to's of ministry without a real deep heart work being done in our lives. Very rarely do we hear messages today that deal with and confront the true motives of our heart by which God will judge everyone and everything. We must not fool ourselves. The human heart is very deceptive (Jer. 17:9). No matter what the pretense, if we are serving God out of selfish motives, we will receive no glory for it.

It is important to catch the spirit of this book. Avoid being overly analytical and placing too much emphasis on minor technicalities and terminology. This writing is by no means exhaustive, but it is a breath from Heaven. Receive it with meekness. It is mildly confrontational, but it has been written in love. Parts of it are pointed and direct to denote urgency.

Please be admonished also that I, your brother and fellow laborer in the work of the Kingdom, am not the son of a "Saul" who has been hurt by a leader. I do not have an axe to grind. This book's ultimate purpose is to save and not destroy. However, it is also to be understood that destruction is sometimes necessary before proper construction can take place. Some will read this book and make changes. They will take serious inventory and reevaluate their lives and motives. Churches and ministries will sway from being "program," "performance," and "platform" based and will return to a "people"-based purpose. Life and fire will be restored to stagnant evangelism that has become prayer-less and passion-less. Some ministries will "downsize" and crucify everything that doesn't bring glory to the Lord. A God-ordained resurrection will undoubtedly follow.

Be warned also that some may not hear this word. They will stiffen their necks and continue on their pathway in their disapproved ministries. Their end and their testimony will be sure and will bear witness to the Scriptures. Their sweet beginning will turn sour in the end (see Mt. 7:21-23).

It is nearly impossible to write a book like this without the judgments of the Lord pressing upon one's own heart. I've done much reflecting upon my own life and ministry. There was a time in my life when my own Bible was "cloudy" and my own love for the Lord and His people were choked by love of programs, performance, and position. I too have been and am being changed.

Leadership is such a precious gift. It expresses the Father's heart to have obedient children, the Lord's desire to guide the scattered sheep, and the Spirit's compulsion to have Jesus glorified in our midst. I do not assume to possess any great gifts of leadership, nor do I have distinguishing credentials to submit to you other than a love and a long-time burden for the purity of Christ's Body and for the restoration of the true spirit of Christianity. May God use this book to fulfill a part of this purpose.

Finally, when this manuscript was ready to go into print, I came across a powerful quote from Watchman Nee that I would like to share with you. These words on leadership were a real confirmation to me concerning the message in this book. Allow the following words to launch you into the ensuing chapters.

"The corrupted old man in the believer has died but his soul remains the power behind his walk. On the one hand the sinful nature has been drastically touched but on the other hand the self life still persists and therefore cannot escape being soulish. To depend upon the soul life to carry out the wish of the

Spirit is to use natural (or human) force to accomplish supernatural (or divine) goodness. This is simply trying to fulfill God's demand with self-strength. Few are those disposed honestly to acknowledge their weakness and incapability and to lean utterly upon God. Who will confess his uselessness if he has not been humbled by the grace of God? Man takes pride in his prowess. He does not understand that however good to the human outlook his efforts may appear to be, they can never please God. He fails miserably to be spiritual and continues to abide in the soul" (Watchman Nee, *The Spiritual Man* [Anaheim, CA: Living Stream Ministry, 1998], Vol. 1-3).

This soulish "self-power" in God's servants must be put to the sword. God's refining fire must burn away this chaff. We must desire nothing but His true glory. As a prophecy that was given several years ago in America stated: "I have used many swords in years past; and some were made of polluted metals. I have used them because they were the only weapons available to Me. But for this last great revival, I must have swords of the purest metals which have been through the hottest fires so that they will not break in My hand."

May God be glorified in the lives of those who desire to serve God with purity of heart. And may God use the solemn word in the pages of this book to keep many from laboring in vain and being disapproved.

Foreword

Bert Farias has written a timely book that is essential reading for everyone in church leadership, as well as for everyone aspiring to leadership and everyone wanting to more fully develop the character of Jesus in their lives. His writing is both convicting and constructive, pointing out the problems with real clarity and then pointing us toward positive, God-glorifying solutions.

You see, the Church will only be as strong as its leaders, and when leaders are insecure, competitive, envious, and worldly—leading out of soulish instincts and motivations instead of leading out of spiritual and biblical principles—then the Church will be fragmented, ineffective, and carnal. The problem is that there is a vicious cycle in which soulish leaders reproduce soulish leaders, and believers seeking to give themselves to effective ministry often have very few godly models to follow.

How can we diagnose this disease in our midst? What are its symptoms and its cure? Chapter after chapter, with real insight and sound use of the Word, Bert exposes the mixed motives and worldly approaches of much contemporary "ministry," contrasting these with the spirit and attitude of Jesus, the ultimate example of biblical leadership.

Of course, you might be wondering by what authority Bert addresses the issue of soulish leadership. Does he write by experience, or is it all theory to him? As one who has known Bert for a good number of years, I can tell you without a doubt that he writes out of personal experience, having proven himself before God and man. He and his wife Carolyn left the comforts of America and labored in impoverished West African nations for nine years, serving another leader's vision the entire time. And, each time the work became sufficiently grounded—a Bible school, churches planted, native workers raised up—Bert turned it over to the nationals. In other words, he never took "ownership" of something that belonged to the Lord, and that is an important key.

Then, just when he was content to labor overseas for the rest of his life, Bert felt God's call to return to America and serve the Church here, helping to equip the saints for action. All of us would do well to take heed to the message of this book—even if it hurts. In the end, if we listen and learn, it will help and heal.

Dr. Michael L. Brown, President
Brownsville Revival School of Ministry

Chapter 1

The Sword of the Lord

For the word of God is quick, and powerful, and sharper than any twoedged sword, piercing even to the dividing asunder of soul and spirit, and of the joints and marrow, and is a discerner of the thoughts and intents of the heart (Hebrews 4:12 KJV).

Quick, powerful, sharp, and piercing shall be the end-time word of the Lord. It will convict and cut, expose and expel, and discern and divide. It will sift men's motives and put pressure on their heart of hearts. In the parable of the wheat and tares, Jesus foretold of a time of harvest when a clear distinction would be made between the seeds and the weeds (see Mt. 13:24-30). We are living in that time.

True seeds are works of the Spirit. Weeds consist of the works that are derived from the soulish scheming of men's minds. True seeds have their origin in Him who is true. Weeds have their roots in selfish ambition; they are sown by those who seek their own glory. True seeds, which bring forth the true Kingdom, sprout from the spirits of those who seek the King's glory. A separation is coming. The sword of the Lord will fall. That which is born of the flesh and the soul will have no place to hide.

Soul and Spirit

In these days God is wanting His Church to walk in His glory and anointing in a greater way and in a greater measure than ever before. In order for that to happen, a separation must be made between the soulish realm (our own will, intellect, and emotions) and the spiritual realm. There must be a separation and a discerning of the thoughts and intents of our hearts so that they might be aligned with the thoughts and intents of God's heart. God's purposes will only be fulfilled by spiritual men who know and understand the mind and the heart of God. Therefore this sifting and separation will begin with leadership.

The key leadership in the Kingdom of God consists of the fivefold ministry gifts. This is the spiritual leadership that God recognizes. These leaders are called to lift people out of their carnal state into a state of spiritual maturity. As long as these leaders operate out of their soulish realm the people will themselves remain in a soulish state. The sheep will always follow the shepherd. This is why when God deals with His people, He will usually begin at the top with leadership. When God stirs, He stirs from the top (Hag. 1:14). When God purges and purifies, He usually begins with His priests, the sons of Levi (Mal. 3:3).

Let's look at a natural example of this principle. How many of you know that God is as intelligent as any employer? If you own a company and assign someone to manage it, who do you go to if there is a problem? Do you go to the manager or to one of the employees? The manager may say, "Well, it's the people. They're not selling. They're not producing. They're late. They're lazy." However, no matter what excuses the manager may offer or what blame he places on the people, the responsibility still rests upon him.

It is the manager's responsibility to see to it that the work is getting done.

Just as the president of a company knows where to go to get results, so does the Lord. God works through the authorities that He has ordained. I believe that God is speaking to His leaders today. As the Body of Christ begins to see spiritual leadership instead of soulish leadership, they will follow.

When Korah led the rebellion with 250 princes of the assembly of Israel against Moses and Aaron, Moses spoke unto them and said:

> ... *"Tomorrow morning the Lord will show who is His and who is holy, and will cause him to come near to Him. That one whom He chooses He will cause to come near to Him"* (Numbers 16:5).

Not everyone who confesses the name of the Lord belongs to Him. Not everyone who grazes our churches on Sunday morning is holy. Not every leader who has a church or ministry, or performs mighty works in the Lord's name, belongs to Him (Mt. 7:21-23). The Lord will show who is really His and who is really holy. Nothing will stand in the way of the pure and holy. Just as God vindicated Moses and Aaron and stood on their side, so will He vindicate His holy servants in this hour. But God is merciful and longsuffering, and the opportunity is now being granted to many to submit to the purging and purification process. We will either depart from iniquity or one day depart from the Lord.

> *Nevertheless the solid foundation of God stands, having this seal: "The Lord knows those who are His," and, "Let everyone who names the name of Christ depart from iniquity"* (2 Timothy 2:19).

Iniquity does not refer just to blatant sins such as adultery or fornication, but it also refers to sins of the heart like jealousy, competition, anger, bitterness, unforgiveness, and strife. It's not the obvious, outward actions of sin that God will deal with most directly in a leader, but the hidden motives of the heart. The quality and quantity of fruit produced is determined by the quality of the soil. The soil is our hearts. The seeds are beneath the soil. Nobody sees them. There are issues in our hearts that are hidden, motives that no one can see except God. These are the most subtle and deadliest types of sin because they defile our spirits. One can repent and forsake exposed, outward sins, but sins of the heart that are hidden and never exposed may never be repented of and forsaken. If not dealt with, these false motives of the heart will result in greater deception and hold their victims in captivity.

Righteous Judgment

As humans, we have a tendency to judge others only by their actions, while we judge ourselves by our good intentions. This is not righteous judgment. Just because a person is bold and confident does not mean that person is proud. Likewise, just because someone is quiet and shy doesn't mean that he's humble. This example can be multiplied many times over in other individuals who by outward appearance may look as if they are sinful but have pure hearts. Similarly, there are those who seem pure by outward appearance, but who are, in fact, full of guile and hypocrisy. One can be wrong in his head and right in his heart. Our words and actions are very important, but they can lie because they don't always line up with our motives and intentions.

Today, many of us would be quick to convict David for his adultery with Bathsheba and murder of Uriah, yet we would acquit Saul of his hidden sin of loving the honor of men more than the honor of God. Like so many of our leaders today, Saul was bound by the fear of man, which is motivated by a love for self. This particular sin of the heart is not as easy to detect. Yet it is deadly and can affect our eternal position and standing with God. It's amazing how many things we do and say to gain the acceptance of men. The result is hypocrisy. Hypocrisy is a great abomination to God because it hinders and kills the move of the Spirit.

God is after truth in the inward parts (Ps. 51:6). He wants Nathanaels who are free of guile and hypocrisy. He wants Daniels whose souls cannot be bought by the flattery and gifts of men. God wants Johns (such as John the Baptist) who are unspoiled by the sophistication of modern-day churches and ministries. He wants Johns (such as John the Beloved) who have their spiritual ears upon the bosom of God and have an understanding of His heart.

God's View of Leadership

God's perspective of things is so different than man's perspective. By appearance, many ministers look very successful, but are total failures in God's eyes. After giving what appeared to be a very large offering, Ananias and Sapphira looked very successful through man's eyes (Acts 5:1-2). If their sin had not been exposed, they would have had the reputation of being among the church's biggest financial contributors. The probable reason they only brought part of the money of the sale of their property and claimed that it was the full amount was they wanted the praise and esteem of men. Nobody was requiring them to give it all (Acts 5:4). Also, did you ever notice how the Lord judged the man Ananias more severely than his wife Sapphira? Sapphira was given a chance to tell the truth. Peter asked her if they had sold the land for "so much" (Acts 5:8). In other words, did the money she had brought represent the total cost of the land? She could have said that it was only a part of it, and her life would have been spared. However, Ananias was not given that same opportunity. He was the head of his household and received a stricter judgment. Heads of households, heads of churches and ministries, beware! This is the reason for this book. If judgment begins in the house of God (1 Pet. 4:17), guess who will go first?

Jesus made Himself of no reputation (Phil. 2:7) and took upon Him the form of a servant. This is the mind that is to be in us. The foundation of all true life and ministry is rooted right here. This attitude is where there is a joining of the Body to the Head. When we attempt to make a name or reputation for ourselves, we cease to be joined to the Head. Jesus is no longer Lord. He is no longer the chief architect and builder of His Kingdom and His Church.

As long as we seek a reputation and a name for ourselves, our wills can never be submitted to God. The will is part of the soul. God gave every man a soul, and the soul is good when it is subject to the Spirit of God. However, when it is outside of God's Spirit and rule, it will dominate us in place of our spirits. That is why Jesus' first requirement for being His disciple is to deny yourself (Mt. 16:24). He demands that from every seeker. Peter was one who forsook everything to follow Jesus, but his soul was still very unharnessed. He had forsaken houses, lands, and family, but he never forsook himself. He possessed a strong, dominating soul that had not yet been subject to the will of God. But once fully submitted to the Lordship of Jesus Christ, even a Peter can be used by God to build His Church.

Chapter 2

How the Lord Builds His Church

And I also say to you that you are Peter, and on this rock I will build My church, and the gates of Hades shall not prevail against it (Matthew 16:18).

The Church that the Lord Jesus Christ builds is a very strong and powerful Church, one that can never be overcome by the forces of hell. But the Church can only be strong and powerful when Jesus builds it, and not man. Before we can know how Jesus builds the Church, we must clearly understand that the Church belongs to Him. Jesus said, "I will build *My* church"; He didn't say that He was going to build *your* church or *your* ministry. The establishment of this truth in one's heart can make the difference between being an honorable or a dishonorable vessel. It can be the difference between being fit or unfit for the Master's use (2 Tim. 2:20-21). A wrong slant on this truth can open the door for the arm of flesh to try to control the Church of God. As shepherds and ministers, we have a responsibility for oversight of the flock of God, but not ownership.

Belonging to God

This simple revelation rooted in your heart determines your response to Jesus. If your approach to the Church is one of ownership, it is guaranteed that you will also try to build it. You will never be able to let go and allow Jesus to build. Do you know why many believers run their own lives? It is because they are not rooted in the revelation that they are not their own (1 Cor. 6:19-20). They have never released ownership of their bodies and their lives to the Lord. That's why there's no abiding power resting upon their lives. Jesus does not inhabit that which He has no control over. In many churches, Jesus has little to no control. In the early Church, however, even their possessions were not counted by the believers as being their own (Acts 4:32). The Lord had full control of their lives and their possessions. The Church was under His Lordship and rule. No wonder there was so much power available to them! Do you see how important it is to release ownership and control to the Lord Jesus and the Spirit of God?

I cannot find too many places in the New Testament where the apostle Paul referred to any of the churches he had planted as his own. Furthermore, in his instructions to younger ministers like Timothy and Titus, he very rarely referred to either the church or the ministry as being their own. Instead he always referred to it as the "church of God" (Acts 20:28; 1 Tim. 3:5). Paul instructed Archippus to take heed to the ministry which he had received in the Lord (Col. 4:17).

Again, Paul exhorted Timothy not to neglect the gift of God that was in him and to stir up the gift of God (1 Tim. 4:14; 2 Tim. 1:6). Peter called us *stewards*, not owners of the manifold grace of God (1 Pet 4:10). These early church leaders had a consciousness and a reverence concerning their gifts and ministries that is sadly lacking in the Church today.

When you take ownership of a gift, a ministry, or a church, there is an element of dependency that is placed on you instead of God. You'll begin to draw people's attention and dependency toward you, sometimes even unconsciously. This will eventually result in undue pressure being placed on you (either by yourself or the people) to perform and produce results. You may even become overly possessive or oppressive in your leadership style—all because of a subtle ownership mentality. There are many ministers today who constantly say, "I'm going to build my church. You are my people. My gift is this. My vision is such and such. My ministry is so and so." This kind of talk subtly and steadily gives access to soulish control.

Jesus: The True Foundation

Now let us see how the Lord builds His Church. He builds it upon the rock, which is the revelation of Jesus as the Christ, the Son of the Living God (Mt. 16:18). The Church is built on the revelation of who He is and the revelation of what He says. Again, Jesus is the pattern Son and our example. In His earthly ministry and walk Jesus only said and did what He heard and saw the Father do (Jn. 5:19,30).

God the Father had revealed Jesus' identity to Peter by the Spirit. And it is upon that revelation that the Lord builds His Church. The greater the personal revelation we have of who Jesus is, the deeper and surer will be the foundation. There has been much discussion in the past few

years concerning the ministry of apostles and prophets.
True apostolic and prophetic ministry has the Lord Jesus as
its focus. Jesus is the centerpiece of all true ministry. He is
to be the cornerstone of all that is built in His name. So
much attention these days has been given to personalities,
projects, and the works of human hands. We worship what
we are beholding. When we behold Jesus, we begin to be
changed into His image and likeness. It's in beholding Him
that we receive His glory. When we as the Church begin to
exalt Jesus more than mere men and programs, we will experience a far greater glory in our midst. The glory is the ev-
idence of the true building process.

John testified of the Lord and drew people's attention to
Him (Jn. 1:26-36). When a question arose among the people concerning purification and how the multitudes were
leaving John and going to Jesus to be baptized, John's reply
in John 3:27-36, especially verses 29-30, put things into
perspective:

*He who has the bride is the bridegroom; but the
friend of the bridegroom, who stands and hears him,
rejoices greatly because of the bridegroom's voice.
Therefore this joy of mine is fulfilled. He must increase, but I must decrease.*

The major part of John's calling was to prepare the bride
to receive the bridegroom. He recognized that the bride belonged to the bridegroom. Oh how we need a revelation of
that today! John referred to himself as a friend of the bridegroom. Today, we have many impostors posing as friends of
the bridegroom, but who are really hindering the bride and
bridegroom from coming together in intimacy. These false
friends are stopping the bridegroom from kissing the bride.

Instead of reconciling men to God, they are reconciling men unto themselves and to their own vision and goals. They are speaking perverse things to draw away disciples after them (Acts 20:30). John the Baptist was not that way, however. He rejoiced that men were going after Jesus and not him. A true friend hears the voice of the bridegroom and rejoices. A false friend rejoices in other voices, especially his own. A true friend's joy is fulfilled when the bridegroom increases and he decreases. A false friend wants to be seen and heard and desires increase for himself.

When our focus is on who we are instead of who He is, there is no glory. The Corinthians were focusing on men and personalities (1 Cor. 1:12), but Paul brought them back to Jesus (1 Cor. 1:23; 2:2). The Corinthians also had a controversy concerning water baptism (1 Cor. 1:13-15). Does this sound familiar? John the Baptist's disciples argued and fussed over the same issues and churches are still fussing over baptisms today. Paul told the Corinthians that he didn't baptize anyone in his own name to make disciples of himself. Isn't it amazing that this great apostle had to defend his ministry and apostleship? These Corinthian Christians misread and misjudged Paul. Sometimes believers have a difficult time discerning a hireling from a true shepherd. The controversy here also seemed to revolve around Apollos because Paul continues to mention him (1 Cor. 3:4-6). Apparently Apollos was a very eloquent man (Acts 18:24), and the Corinthians seemed to have a soulish attraction to him. I believe that is why Paul included in his letter a discourse about not trusting in the wisdom of men, but trusting in the power of God (1 Cor. 1:18–2:5). He went on to say that the only true foundation to build upon was Jesus Christ, and we must be careful how we build (1 Cor. 3:10-11). We must have a revelation of who He is and glory in Him.

Second, we must have a revelation of what He says. The apostle Peter not only received a revelation of who Jesus was, but he also received the revelation of the words of Jesus.

But Simon Peter answered Him, "Lord, to whom shall we go? You have the words of eternal life" (John 6:68).

Every spiritual house is built by walking in the wisdom of what has been revealed to us by God (Prov. 9:1). A spiritual house can be a church, a ministry, or one's personal life. The Lord Jesus cannot build His Church upon what is revealed by flesh and blood or by the wisdom of men. Rather, He builds it upon our obedience to what He reveals and says, not only in the written Word, but also what is being said or revealed to us by His Spirit. Maximum yield comes to those who hear and obey. We need to pray consistently, hear from God consistently, and obey and follow Him consistently, especially as leaders. This is the way the Lord builds strong lives, strong families, strong ministries, and strong churches.

The Leader's Mandate

When David Yonggi Cho, pastor of one of the world's largest churches, was asked about the secret of his success in ministry, he replied by saying, "I pray and I obey." This must be the top priority of every leader and minister. When it is not, then we dishonor our priestly ministry, and by our own negligence, place our ministry on a lower level. God is looking for ministers with His heart and mind who will take time to hear from Him. These ministers are true spiritual leaders.

> *Then I will raise up for Myself a faithful priest who shall do according to what is in My heart and in My mind. I will build him a sure house, and he shall walk before My anointed forever* (1 Samuel 2:35).

Notice again that it is God who raises up faithful priests (ministers) and builds sure houses. God wants faithful priests and ministers who will do everything that is in His heart and mind, not what is in their hearts and minds. Doing things "according to God's heart and mind" simply means following His plan and vision for our lives and ministries. The Lord will then be the chief architect and master builder, not you. The apostle Paul referred to himself as a wise master builder, but only after declaring that he and others were laborers together with God, and that the Church belonged to God (1 Cor. 3:9-10). Paul did not have an ownership mentality of the Church or the people, and he realized that he labored with God and not apart from Him, His plan, and His purpose. Understanding this qualified him as a wise master builder. You see, in one sense we are builders, but we are builders together with God. Laboring together with God signifies working with His plan and purpose, in His strength and grace, not our own. That's the reason Paul cautions us, by the Spirit of God, on how we build.

It's very easy to labor and build apart from God's heart and mind. It's easy to do things our own way and even for our own purpose. Our motives can be very easily tainted with selfish aspirations. Regardless of how many times we may say, "All the glory goes to God," if we are building for ourselves, our works will suffer the judgment of God. The works that have their origin in who Christ is and in what He says are gold, silver, and precious stones; but those which have their origin in our souls and natural thinking are wood, hay, and stubble. The fire of God will try them both (1 Cor. 3:13). Will your works stand the test?

Chapter 3

Whose Kingdom
Are You Building?

So on a set day Herod, arrayed in royal apparel, sat on his throne and gave an oration [speech] to them. And the people kept shouting, "The voice of a god and not of a man!" Then immediately an angel of the Lord struck him, because he did not give glory to God. And he was eaten by worms and died (Acts 12:21-23).

This same type of scenario happens today. The people were looking to Herod, a mere man, for answers instead of God. In today's Christian world we can see many ministries built around a man and his personality. In many cases, if these men were to die, their ministries and/or churches would not stand. If a ministry is built upon a man and not upon God, it will not last.

Where Is the Focus?

I believe that many of us as today's leaders have portrayed an image to the people such as King Herod did. We dress in the finest clothes, we wear the finest jewelry, we have the newest hairstyles, and we drive the fanciest cars.

All this adds to our charisma. None of these things are entirely wrong in themselves, but we need to be careful that we are not drawing attention to ourselves. These things do attract people; however, we must realize that this type of image appeals to the soul of man and not the spirit. This soulish appeal often results in people giving too much credence to a man. People will begin to say the exact same thing in their hearts as those in the Book of Acts said about Herod: "It is the voice of a god, and not of a man."

This soulish appeal causes many to begin to lift up these ministers. They may not vocalize their thoughts, but inside they're saying, "Look at him (or her). Look at the way he walks. See how eloquent he is." In their hearts they begin to develop a god-image of this minister, and they begin to worship a personality instead of Jesus. You know what happened to Herod. He was smitten by the angel of the Lord, eaten up of worms, and died. Think about that for awhile.

This account in Acts describes what happened to Herod. However, his example holds true for much of our leadership today. Such showy outward-oriented leadership is soulish; it appeals to the emotional realm. Our churches have become theaters, and our ministers actors, while the peoples' tithes and offerings serve as the gate fees. Although there are many renowned ministries that are legitimately serving God, there are also many that seem to be putting showmanship above servanthood, and hype above the leading and work of the Holy Spirit. It's time for many of us to do some serious self-examination.

Once again, this entire teaching rests upon the difference between the spirit and the soul. I believe that some churches and ministries today are dangerously centered around one person. The Body of Christ needs to work as a team. It needs to be a corporate effort. That is what will get the job done—not one person! This is what we were privileged to see as missionaries in Africa for a number of years. What began ten years ago in one nation with six adult missionaries has now, at this writing, spread to over 15 African nations with churches and works that are now mostly under national leadership. Was this great growth due to how anointed we were? No, but it happened only because we learned to "let go and let God." There was an equipping and a mobilizing of the saints to do the work of the ministry, and it was the result of a team of ministers working under a corporate anointing. The hand of God will always rest upon that type of ministry. Conversely, the Lord's hand is being removed from the one-man-show type of ministry. "Why?" you may ask. Because they will not give God the glory.

*And the Lord said to Gideon, "The people who are with you are too many for Me to give the Midianites into their hands, **lest Israel claim for itself against Me**, saying, 'My own hand has saved me' "* (Judges 7:2).

*But Gideon said to them, "**I will not rule over you**, nor shall my son rule over you; **the Lord shall rule over you**"* (Judges 8:23).

"Although Gideon wisely refused to serve as king of Israel upon his death, his son Abimelech hired assassins to murder his brothers, in hope of seizing rule for himself. His youngest brother, Jotham, who escaped, climbed Mount Gerizim and prophesied that a kingdom founded on sin would soon shatter; and within three years this happened. Gideon understood that

God intended Israel to be a theocracy (God is King); but Abimelech, though possessing a natural charisma, did not have the mind of God, His appointment, or His anointing. Godly leaders do things God's way. Doing things man's way disqualifies men from leading. The leader who seeks to benefit himself at the expense of others will be stamped with God's disapproval. Unlike his humble father, Abimelech was ambitious, believing the end justified the means. God judges leaders not on how much they accomplish, but on whether they do things God's way" ("Kingdom Dynamics," *Spirit-Filled Life Bible*, [Nashville: Thomas Nelson, 1991], 360).

In reality, there are two types of ministries or churches today: the Lord's and man's. Either God is building it, or He's not. When a ministry trains, equips, and sends forth laborers, taking the focus off of one person and his or her importance to the ministry's success, then greater increase comes. This is what we saw happen in our years in Africa. This proves that the ministry's success was not due to any one particular person. Rather, it was God who gave the increase.

Servant-Leader or King?

Leadership is not building a kingship image in the eyes of the people. In other words, leaders are not to rule the people, but to lead them. If you will look back to the Old Testament, you will find that it was never God's intention or desire for Israel to have Saul as a king. Unfortunately, the charismatic world has had charismatic kings; kings to whom people bow down in their hearts. Most people will not admit to this because they know that it's wrong. Yet in their hearts, they say, "Aren't they wonderful? I love to hear that person speak. Oh, they're so anointed!" By doing this, they make the minister out to be an idol. Israel wanted a king instead of God's leadership. Today people still insist on making kings out of ministerial personalities. It is hero worship and a subtle rejection of God's rule and reign.

> *But the thing displeased Samuel when they said, "Give us a king to judge us." So Samuel prayed to the Lord. And the Lord said to Samuel, "Heed the voice of the people in all that they say to you; for they have not rejected you, but they have rejected Me, that I should not reign over them"* (1 Samuel 8:6-7).

The Lord told Samuel that the people's request for a king was actually a rejection of Him and His reign over them. Either God reigns or man reigns; both cannot reign at the same time. The Lord granted their request. However, He instructed Samuel to tell the people what would happen when their desires were fulfilled. There is a great lesson for us to learn in this.

> *So Samuel told all the words of the Lord to the people who asked him for a king. And he said, "This will be the behavior of the king who will reign over you: He will take your sons and appoint them for **his** own chariots and to be **his** horsemen; and some will run before **his** chariots. He will appoint captains over **his** thousands and captains over **his** fifties, will set some to plow **his** ground and reap **his** harvest, and some to make **his** weapons of war and equipment for **his** chariots* (1 Samuel 8:10-12).

Samuel told the people that a king would build *his* kingdom. He went on to tell them how much that a king would take from them. Never forget, a king builds *his* kingdom, not God's. He will use any means to justify the building of *his* kingdom. This is often an unspoken attitude of the heart that exists in ministry. It manifests in a selfishness toward one's own ministry or church. It will not esteem another church or ministry before its own. Notice that the king would have "*his* chariots [vehicles for ministry]...*his* horsemen [those who steer those vehicles]...*his* ground [territory]...*his* harvest [souls in *his* territory]...*his* weapons of war, and equipment for *his* chariots [tools and resources for ministry]." How many have been guilty of the very same attitude in ministry, using everyone and everything to build their kingdoms instead of letting God build His?

Chapter 4

True Ministry
Versus False Ministry

True ministry: A ministry in which the different members of the body all have contributing parts; a ministry which is a means to an end and not an end in and of itself.

False ministry: A ministry in which the minister has the "me, my, and mine" attitude; a ministry in which the importance is placed on the building and establishing of the minister's ministry.

Remember these two definitions, and don't confuse the two. We are to test the spirits to determine whether they are of God (1 Jn. 4:1). Anyone can be fooled by outward forms and demonstrations of so-called ministry. The spirit of a ministry is more important than its doctrine. The differences between true and false ministry are based on the spirit of that ministry.

True Ministry

True ministry produces inclusion, incorporation, and partnership. False ministry produces exclusion, isolation, and competition. Probably every major revival or move of

God has died because of the manifestation of a wrong spirit. True ministry desires to include everyone who has been washed in the blood of Jesus. It recognizes its need for the other parts of the Body. It shows no partiality, and it is willing to network and partner with others in the Body of Christ. On the other hand, false ministry (often because of race, color, denominational labels, or petty doctrinal differences) will disjoin itself from others and even prohibit its members from associating with the same. It will isolate itself in the name of "preserving true doctrine" or having a different ministry style or vision. Sadly, the more these ministries isolate themselves, the more disconnected they become from the true heart of God.

Let's see how God intended true ministry to work:

Everyone helped his neighbor, and said to his brother, "Be of good courage!" So the craftsman encouraged the goldsmith; he who smooths with the hammer inspired him who strikes the anvil, saying, "It is ready for the soldering"; then he fastened it with pegs, that it might not totter (Isaiah 41:6-7).

This is a striking passage of idolatry, but it can be related to show how team ministry is supposed to work. Notice how the different parts, abilities, and gifts work together. They are all contributing to the common vision and purpose of God. They encourage one another. True ministry builds bridges, not barriers. It builds up, not tears down. It lightens, not darkens. It unites, not divides. It doesn't wish for its brother's failure, but for his success. It also contributes to that success because it realizes that we are all on the same team.

We cannot afford to build our own little temporal kingdoms (temporal, meaning that which will be destroyed) when God's big eternal purpose and plan are awaiting fulfillment. However, it is true that there are men striving to build their kingdoms, their churches, and their ministries. One can often see these people at large conferences handing out their ministry cards. They're exchanging addresses. They're looking for the biggest pastors of the biggest churches in order to get the biggest offerings so that they can have the "biggest" ministry. God does not need us or our big ministries. Rather, He has chosen us, and we are privileged to share in the joy of His labor. God will not share His glory with anyone. All that is not glorious will one day be destroyed. Churches and ministries need to be built on His glory and for His glory.

False Ministry

A false ministry will mirror the characteristics discussed in the last chapter. Obviously, the building of one's own ministry takes priority, but one can also pinpoint a false ministry by the way it treats its people. Under a false ministry people are oppressed, not liberated; they are made joyless, not joyful. A false ministry will use and control its people.

*He will **take** your daughters to be perfumers, cooks, and bakers* (1 Samuel 8:13).

*...He will **take**...for himself.... And he will **take**...And he will **take**...And he will **take**...He will **take**....* (1 Samuel 8:11,14,15,16,17 KJV).

Can anything be clearer than these passages of Scripture? False ministry uses people to build its kingdom and its ministry or church. False ministry takes advantage of people. How do you feel when your children are taken advantage of? How do you suppose God feels when His children are treated in the same way? Attempting to advance at another's expense will one day reap dire consequences. True ministry attempts to advance another at its own expense. That's what Calvary is all about. True ministry takes from itself to give to others.

*Did I make a gain of you by any of them whom I sent unto you? I desired Titus, and with him I sent a brother. Did Titus make a **gain** of you? walked we not in the same **spirit**? walked we not in the same **steps**?* (2 Corinthians 12:17-18 KJV)

True spiritual leadership will not take advantage of the people; rather, it seeks their gain. A true leader desires to help others fulfill *God's* will and plan for their lives, not the *leader's* will and plan for them. It doesn't matter what amount of ability and faithfulness someone may possess. If they are not called to be a part of the church or ministry you lead, then you don't want them no matter how much you think you need them. And when it is time for them to leave, for heaven's sake, let them leave. They need to fulfill their destiny in God, not your destiny for them.

Note also that the same spirit and steps that the apostle Paul portrayed were reflected among those on his ministry team. Spiritual steps do not walk on or over people, but they walk ahead and lead by example. The spirit and the steps of a leader will likely be the same that those under that leadership will take. That is why it is so important to always convey a right spirit to those being led. It is even possible to say all the right words with the wrong spirit. People have a tendency to respect leadership, and they will listen to a leader even when his spirit is wrong because they respect the leader's words. Leaders must watch the motive behind their words.

Let me share an example from our missionary experience in Africa. There are ministers today who are traveling throughout Africa and around the world whose spirits have done much damage to the Body of Christ. They are promoting race, gender, and nationality above the Spirit of God. They say that they have a calling to lift certain cultures and races out of their oppression. That sounds like a noble cause, right? But they are doing so at the expense and exclusion of all other races who are in the Body of Christ and have the same spirit of Christ. I personally heard one of these men say that certain Third World peoples should not take used clothing from America and that they should also reject any foreign aid. He said that this particular people group are better than that. He went on to say that they shouldn't even take canned sardines because there are fresh fish right off the seashore. In fact, in his opinion, no one should eat sardines at all. He may say that this approach is intended to make the Third World church self-sufficient and indigenous, but by acting in this way, he is dividing, offending, and hurting other races, especially missionaries, at the expense of the blood of Jesus Christ which makes us one. I know from first-hand exposure to some of the proponents of this teaching that it breeds arrogance and pride in those who adhere to it. Its fruit is exclusion, isolation, and competition. Regardless of the words that are used to describe or justify it, the spirit of this message is giving birth to bad fruit. Therefore, it must be clearly identified as false ministry. He who is a true Christian does not glory in himself, his color, race, church, or ministry, but glories in the Lord.

Chapter 5

Humility

Do nothing out of selfish ambition or vain conceit, but in humility ["lowliness of mind," KJV] consider others better than yourselves. Each of you should look not only to your own interests, but also to the interests of others (Philippians 2:3-4 NIV).

Let this mind be in you which was also in Christ Jesus, who, being in the form of God, did not consider it robbery to be equal with God, but made Himself of no reputation, taking the form of a bondservant, and coming in the likeness of men. And being found in appearance as a man, He humbled Himself and became obedient to the point of death, even the death of the cross (Philippians 2:5-8).

Christ's Example

A right spirit and a right heart are everything in life and ministry. The hallmark of a right life is the spirit of humility. The only spiritual posture that the grace of God can flow into is the humble heart. Humility has very little to do with outward poses or postures, but it has everything to do with the position of the heart. As stated earlier, God-confident people are often accused of being proud, while the quiet and reserved are labeled as humble. This, however, is not always the case. How then can one identify true humility? Following are five characteristics of humility from the above verses:

1. It makes itself of no reputation.
2. It takes upon itself the form of a servant.
3. It possesses lowliness of mind.
4. It esteems others better than themselves.
5. It is obedient to God at all costs.

Humility is a conforming of our wills to the will of God. This means that our lives are an altar before God and not a throne. Are you building your life as an altar or a throne? If you are on an altar dedicated to God, then you are embracing that which is more beneficial to others than yourself. You esteem others better than yourself. Instead of taking the chief seat, you take the low seat. Your spiritual posture is not of one waiting to be served, but of one who serves. If you are on a self-made throne, you are embracing that which is more beneficial to you than to others. The Lord Jesus laid down His own will all the way to Calvary. He lived every day of his life for someone else. He was obedient even unto the death of the cross. He was lowly in heart and lowly in mind. What an example of a Savior!

Walk in Humility Each Day

It is virtually impossible to be completely delivered of spiritual pride. It is always bidding for residential rights to our hearts and lives. Unbeknownst to us, it is rather easy to fall into a most subtle deception where God actually becomes our servant instead of our Master. We make our own plans and ask God to bless them. We design our own course of action and ask God to remove the obstacles. We pray for

God to do what we need for Him to do so that our lives can be better and happier. This is all due to a lack of understanding of who God is and who we are in relation to Him. The wrong perspective of God in our lives will always result in idolatry, which simply means that we serve God our own way.

Humility is attractive to God and to spiritual people. It is the one attribute that makes all the others. If one does not detect a true spirit of humility in positions of leadership, he should be very careful. Humility is honest, transparent, and pure. It will admit when it's wrong. It will ask to be forgiven (when was the last time you witnessed a leader asking for forgiveness?). It will also forgive. And here's a big one: It does not seek a reputation, except to be like Christ who made Himself of no reputation. There is so much of this in all of us that we are not even aware of. Are you dead to the influence of men? Totally dead? Does it matter to you what people think of you? We all want to be accepted, right? We all want to be liked and esteemed by our peers, right? When it honestly doesn't matter to you any more, then you are getting close to a major deliverance.

A mighty prayer warrior who lived in the 1800's was asked one day by the Spirit of God not to wear his hat to town. This was a great humiliation because in his day all decent men wore their hats in public. It was their custom. This man and his family were highly respected people of that town. However, the reason the Lord wanted him to do this was so that he could gain complete victory over the influence of men. This man of God wrestled with just the thought of it and of the awful disgrace that it would bring to his parents, family, and friends. He finally obeyed and set out for town. The Lord made him a spectacle, and he said it seemed as if all the forces of hell were attacking this simple act of obedience. Other severe tests of humility and obedience followed in this man's life. Yet God gave him victory and honored his obedience through these trials. How great are the depths of our desires to be accepted and respected in this world! We must be stripped.

This is one of the chief reasons why men are so driven to be successful both in life and ministry. It is not altogether wrong to want to be respected, but when it affects one's obedience to God, it becomes a problem. Overly self-conscious people are some of God's prime targets for deliverance from respectability. Many times in a church service these people will refrain from shouting, jumping, running, or dancing because they do not want to lose their sense of dignity. Sometimes people question the purpose of such manifestations, but many times it serves to deliver these individuals from the influence of men. We will never walk in the fullness of our God-given authority until we are free of every influence of man. Humility is the gateway to greater authority, freedom, and effectiveness in life and ministry.

Don't Lose Your Way

I remember hearing the testimony of an older minister. When the organization he founded began to grow, his board of directors came to him and asked him to consider upgrading to a classier automobile. The reason, they said, was to upgrade this minister's image. The minister said, "No, I like my Chevrolet." They said, "Brother, you don't understand. The work and the ministry are growing, and we want to get you a vehicle that will correlate with the ministry God has given you." The minister quickly shot back, "No, you don't understand. I like my Chevrolet, and I will continue to drive my Chevrolet!" I thank God for this minister's spunk. I am certainly not opposed to ministers driving nice cars, but if they are doing so merely to enhance their image and the public's esteem of them, then that minister has just departed from the faith.

One of the saddest stories in Scripture is the life of King Saul. Here was a man who seemingly started out so humble, but eventually lost his way completely. There are many people who start out strong in God only to finish weakly or never finish at all. Let's look at Saul's beginning and use him as an example of what can happen when one develops a wrong motivation for ministry.

> ... *"Am I not a Benjamite, of the smallest of the tribes of Israel, and my family the least of all the families of the tribe of Benjamin? Why then do you speak like this to me?"* (1 Samuel 9:21)

> *When he had caused the tribe of Benjamin to come near by their families, the family of Matri was chosen. And Saul the son of Kish was chosen. But when they sought him, he could not be found. Therefore they inquired of the Lord further, "Has the man come here yet?" And the Lord answered, "There he is, hidden among the equipment"* (1 Samuel 10:21-22).

As you can see, Saul had a very small estimation of himself when he started out. When it came time for him to present himself before the people, he was in hiding. When he finally appeared, the Bible says that he stood head and shoulders above everyone, and the prophet Samuel testified that there was none like Saul among the people (1 Sam. 10:23-24). Yet Saul didn't see himself that way. He was small in his own eyes (1 Sam. 15:17). When certain men despised his ministry at its conception, Saul even held his peace (1 Sam. 10:27). He didn't defend himself or fight back. It appears that he had a very humble beginning. However, after failing a series of tests from the Lord, his heart began to change. He began to honor the opinion of man over his esteem of God. David's success caused Saul to grow jealous of him. The more the Lord honored and prospered David, the more hatred and jealousy Saul developed toward him. This attitude prevailed throughout Saul's life. Instead of building the Kingdom of God, Saul became obsessed with protecting and keeping his own kingdom, and the killing and disposing of another man became the means to do it. We can harbor murder in our hearts toward fellow ministers without ever committing the physical act. A spirit of envy, jealousy, and competition will lead to hatred, which is the same as murder. Are we truly glad when others succeed in ministry?

The Spirit of Saul

I believe the spirit of Saul is perhaps the greatest hindrance to revival in our churches and in our land. It is prominent in much of our leadership. Because of this prevailing spirit, there are times when I wanted to draw away completely from ministry and return to secular work. There are other times when I sense it trying to raise its ugly head in my own heart, and it sickens me. Rather than hate our brothers and fellow ministers, we need to learn to hate this spirit of Saul that can overtake any one of us if we are not careful. Let me give you a modern-day example that happened to a minister whom I knew quite well. This man was pastoring a church overseas, and he felt in his heart the need to be on the road traveling stateside, ministering and raising funds for the work overseas. Therefore, he let one of his associates pastor the church of about 100 people, most of whom were nationals. In a short time, under this other man's leadership, the church grew to 1,000 people. The nationals were being trained and discipled. They were being mobilized and sent forth to minister. The Spirit of God was moving and good things were happening.

One day this other head man called his associate into his office and said, "I appreciate what you have done. God has used you to cause the church to grow. But I need to be back in the pulpit. I don't want to travel much anymore. The people need to see me in that pulpit. I need to be the center of it." I asked the man who related this story to me, a very reliable source, if these were his exact words: "I need to be the center of it." I listened in utter disbelief as the man assured me that they were. I asked him again, "Are you sure? Did you hear this with your own ears?" He responded once more affirmatively. Then he added more shocking words. He said that this head man went on to say, "I would rather have the church be 100 people with me being the center of it than 1,000 people and me not being the center of it." I've heard it said, "Some people would rather be number one in hell than number two in Heaven." I asked the man who related this story to me what happened. He told me that he believed this leader experienced the same as Saul, that an evil spirit came and oppressed him. I don't know what the condition of this man is today. He may now be free. But I do know that this spirit of jealousy and competition has marked this contemporary age of so-called ministry.

God anointed Saul and placed His Spirit upon him and changed him into another man (1 Sam. 10:6). God also touched the hearts of men to help and support Saul in ministry (1 Sam. 10:26). It was God's grace that equipped Saul for ministry.

Know Your Source

…"A man can receive nothing unless it has been given to him from heaven" (John 3:27).

For who regards you as superior? And what do you have that you did not receive? But if you did receive it, why do you boast as if you had not received it? (1 Corinthians 4:7 NAS)

If Heaven has given us something, how can we boast of it as if we've received it by our own strength, wisdom, and ability? Why do we boast of our ministries as if we built them by our own power (maybe some of us have)? Who called us and anointed us? Who has given us grace? Imagine what would have happened if, during Jesus' triumphant entry into Jerusalem when the people were shouting praises, the donkey had thought that these praises were for him. We can persuade ourselves into thinking that we are really something. Yet no man can boast of his own measure against another. The Scriptures tell us it is unwise to compare ourselves with others. There are different graces given to individuals for different operations (Eph. 4:11; 1 Cor. 12:28). There are different emphases on different ministries and churches. Much of the striving in ministry comes from comparison. It then leads us to have unsanctified ambition, which causes us to produce or manifest something that God has not given. This is often the cause of much disorder and confusion in ministry.

For wherever there is jealousy (envy) and contention (rivalry and selfish ambition), there will also be confusion (unrest, disharmony, rebellion) and all sorts of evil and vile practices (James 3:16 AMP).

The itch for publicity and popularity is a widespread disease among ministers. God has distributed His grace and gifts to each of us across His Body so that we can each make a contribution to bless others. Don't try to be more than what God has made you. Don't attempt to contribute more than God has distributed. Appreciate the contributions of others, even if they seem to have a greater impact than yours. And if you regard yourself as having a ministry of great impact, esteem the contributions of others greater than your own. Do not have bitter envying and strife in your heart, especially as it relates to ministry. Instead, rejoice in the fact that you are a new creation in Christ Jesus and a privileged co-laborer with God. When you do, you'll begin to experience the peace of God again in your life and ministry.

Now here is a prescription for receiving full deliverance from rivalry and contention in your heart against other leaders and ministers. Pastors, go and bless other pastors with that which you want for yourself. Missionaries, go and bless other missionaries with the thing you'd most like someone to do for you. Traveling ministers, go and do the same for another traveling minister. Don't complain, compare, or compete, but rejoice, show care, and be sweet. Go find someone who's discouraged and hurting and lift him up. That's where you will find the presence of God.

Chapter 6

The Operation of the Soul

Therefore if the whole church comes together in one place, and all speak with tongues, and there come in those who are uninformed or unbelievers, will they not say that you are out of your mind? But if all prophesy, and an unbeliever or an uninformed person comes in, he is convinced of all, he is convicted by all. And thus the secrets of his heart are revealed; and so, falling down on his face, he will worship God and report that God is truly among you (1 Corinthians 14:23-25).

The apostle Paul, by the Spirit of God, is writing to the church at Corinth. He is simply doing what every good minister should be constantly doing, which is to pull young believers out of the soulish operation of these spiritual gifts and into the Spirit. These believers in Corinth were soulish Christians. They were operating these gifts in the soulish realm without understanding their full purpose.

Though the gifts of the Spirit are accurate, we are often inaccurate in flowing in the operation of them. These gifts are perfect, but they flow through imperfect vessels. And, really, if we're not careful, our brand of Christianity can be almost entirely soulish. We can walk or operate completely out of emotion and our natural minds.

Prayer

Our prayer lives can be soulish. Prayer is good and prayer is right, but we need to learn how to pray accurately by the Spirit of God. When prayer is not accurate, it becomes soulish. We begin to pray things out only by emotion. We pray only when we're in some kind of crisis or trouble. We pray our own agenda instead of God's agenda. Many times circumstances will dictate the way we pray. If we're not careful, the devil will get into that emotional and circumstantial arena, and he will indirectly begin to dictate the way that we pray. But when we learn to pray accurately and by the Spirit, we'll be out ahead of the devil. When we pray by the Spirit, we pray prophetically into the future, and then we walk according to our prayers.

Worship

Our times of corporate praise and worship can be soulish. Again, one can be operating strictly out of the mind and emotion. We tap our feet and sway our bodies to the music. We clap our hands to the music. Then when the music stops, we're finished. Now music enhances the anointing and presence of God, but, on the other hand, I've seen people dance in the Spirit without any music. Sometimes we can do things just because of the music. If the music is fast and upbeat, we think we're in the Spirit; but if it's slow, we don't feel anything. How many times have we witnessed this? During the fast praise songs the people may become really excited, but then when it comes time to enter into deeper worship, it takes so long for people to enter in. Why does it work this way? It's because most people don't live there. They walk and live in their soul.

Preaching and Ministry

The preaching and teaching of the Word of God can be soulish. Again, the Word is pure and perfect, but we are not. As ministers, it can become very easy for us to minister the Word of God after the seeing of the natural eye or the hearing of the natural ear. In our preaching, we can deal with problems after the flesh through knowing and recognizing people and events in the natural. We can preach things that we know will appeal to and excite people's souls and emotions. We may preach certain messages because we don't want to offend anyone. And (here's a big one) we can minister and preach out of our own hurts and offenses. These are some things that can make the ministry of the Word of God soulish.

Moreover, much of what we call ministry, such as altar calls for salvation, the laying on of hands for healing or deliverance, or other forms of ministration can be done soulishly. Now the soul is not bad. It was given to us by God. In its rightful place of subjection to God's Spirit, the soul can be very powerful. But when it works apart from the influence of the Spirit of God, at best, it becomes an imitator and a performer of what it thinks God is doing. We get ourselves in trouble when we try to perform in the name of ministry. In our attempt to move where God is not moving we can even give ourselves over to seducing, psychic, and familiar spirits.

God Does the Work

And being fully convinced that what He had promised He was also able to perform (Romans 4:21).

Who does the performing? We hear ministers often say: "We got 1,000 people saved at our crusade, or we got ten crippled people healed. I got 100 people filled with the Holy Ghost." No, you didn't. We cannot take credit for anything. God performs these things as we obey Him, and many times, God just does it on His own without us. This is an important attitude to maintain in ministry. Because of the soulish desire to succeed and see something supernatural manifest, people often move from the true operation of the Spirit and into the soul. They will begin to push and strive, trying to make something happen. That's a dangerous place to be because it is at that point you find yourself striving against God and His plan.

How many times have you prayed for a sick person and believed God for a miracle? I've taken people's crooked limbs in my hands and tried to make them straight myself. I've wanted people to be healed so badly that I would attempt to do anything that I thought could aid in their healing. Many times when they were not healed, I became frustrated and questioned the Lord about it. It was at these times that the Lord would just tell me that I didn't know everything about the person or the situation of his heart and life. Of course, it could've been my own unbelief, or that of the congregation, which hindered the manifestation of the healing. There are reasons why people fail to receive. Sometimes God will tell you, and other times He won't. Sometimes you'll be able to help people and sometimes you won't. But the important thing, and the point that I want to emphasize here, is that a person is not the performer.

Ministers often take the principles of faith, healing, or authority and enter into the arena of the soul to try to make it happen. That's how ministers get into gimmicks. That's why ministers will sometimes push the people down who are standing in the prayer lines because they want others to know that God is really moving and things are happening. Most of the time I believe this happens because of impure motives and a strong desire to be successful in the public eye. Other times I believe it's because there is a genuine desire in the ministers to really see people blessed and helped. Sometimes these attempts to perform can also backfire on us and actually hinder people from receiving the true ministry of the Spirit.

For example, one time a good minister friend of mine and his wife were believing God for healing in their bodies. They didn't tell anyone, but just put their total trust in God. They went to a meeting and purposed in their hearts that when the minister laid hands on them for healing, they would receive their healing. They sat on the front row and heard the message on healing. The minister used examples in his preaching that were a confirmation to this couple for their healing. When the altar call was given they were the first two up there. They were ready to receive. The minister first laid hands on my friend's wife. He pushed her head back and said, "You're not receiving!" Well, what did he mean? He meant, as we'll see shortly, that she wasn't falling down. He equated falling down with being healed. (Now there is a falling down or a "slaining" in the Spirit that is a true and genuine manifestation of God. We are speaking here of a soulish counterfeit.)

My minister friend was standing next to his wife, and he heard and saw all of this. He desperately wanted to receive with his spirit and stay out of the natural realm. As soon as my friend was touched, he went down. He wasn't down on the floor for two seconds before one of the ushers grabbed him underneath the arm and jerked him off the floor. The usher told him that he needed to sit down because they wanted to get other people to the front to be ministered to. Do you think that my friend or his wife got their healing? Not on that day, they didn't. Healing comes out of the spiritual realm and then works itself out into your body. Due to the soulish operations of this minister and his ushers, my friend and his wife were actually pulled out of the spirit and hindered from receiving their healing.

Meanwhile, the congregation was clapping, thinking that it was the anointing because people were falling down. In reality, it was nothing more than emotion, hype, and a mockery of the true operation of the Spirit of God. The soul of man was busy imitating the true move of God. What appeared to be God was not God at all. This frequently happens in services. Meetings are hyped to project that something is really happening. We'll cover more of this issue in a later chapter.

Grow in Strength and Spirit

As previously stated, if we're not careful our entire Christian life and walk can be soulish. For instance, if we obey God *only* when our emotions are high and everything is wonderful, we actually lose strength. Mountaintop experiences are not where we grow strong spiritually. If we only pray, rejoice, forgive, and love when we feel like it, we give access for our souls and emotions to have control of our lives. Our spirits are strengthened in adversity if we keep our joy. It's when we go through tests and trials rejoicing that we grow stronger. God is not so much interested in getting us out of our crisis as He is in strengthening our spirits.

I'm saying all this because I, for one, am concerned that much of the Church is not cut out to endure end-time hardship. We know something about "family" but very little about "army." We have few soldiers in the army of God who are fit to fight. Much of the Church needs to regain the warfare mentality that is so depictive of the entire Christian life. Suffice it to say for now that in order to birth a new breed of Christian soldier, we need a new breed of training. We have a mandate, especially as ministers, to develop strong spiritual Christians by pulling them out of the soul and into the spirit.

> *Now when they heard this, they were cut to the heart, and said to Peter and the rest of the apostles, "Men and brethren, what shall we do?"* (Acts 2:37)

Note the expression "cut to the heart." What caused the cutting? What caused the penetration of the Word of God into their hearts? Wasn't it the anointing of God? It was the active, energizing, and living Word of God. It was the sword of the Spirit that separated the souls of these people from their spirits. It was the transference of the fire and conviction of the Spirit of God. That is what moved these people to respond and act on what they heard. Many times preachers struggle to gain a positive response from their congregations. Many times people are not moved to action. They are not motivated in their hearts to submit completely to God. We need less soulish activity and more spiritual activity in our lives, ministries, and churches. In our prayer and worship, in our preaching and teaching, in the operation of the gifts of the Spirit, and in the ministration to the people, we need to call out to God for a greater supply of His Spirit. Then we need to let God be God and learn to flow with Him.

And thus the secrets of his heart are revealed; and so, **falling down on his face**, *he will worship God and report that God is truly among you* (1 Corinthians 14:25).

This is what will happen more and more frequently when we get over into the Spirit. Instead of having so many people falling backward, we will have people falling forward and submitting to God.

Chapter 7

Three Things
That Make Us Soulish

My wife and I were missionaries in West Africa for a number of years, and we worked closely with a number of pastors and ministers there. The experience was both educating and revealing for us. We learned some things in ministry about what to do, and much of the time, what not to do. We made some mistakes and learned from them. But we also learned much by watching other ministers make mistakes. It was during these earlier years of ministry that we first began to witness firsthand the incredible amount of envy, jealousy, and competition that can sometimes exist among ministries and churches.

The Lord called us to work with other missionaries to establish interdenominational Bible training centers. That was our assignment in Africa. This involved working with and relating to many pastors and also training younger ministers. It is our testimony today that everywhere we went God moved and blessed our endeavors. However, it was not without much opposition. That is to be expected. What surprised us, and what we didn't expect at first, was from whom the opposition would come. The most fierce opposition came, not from the Muslims, the witchdoctors, or the pagan crowd, but from the churches. And many times, it wasn't from the "religious" and traditional churches, but from Bible-believing and full-gospel churches and pastors.

Here is the typical scenario that occurred in almost every country and city God would send us. We would visit churches and meet the pastors. We would share the vision God gave us for starting a training center in their city. When the school began, we had students from many different churches and backgrounds. However, when the anointed Word of God began to birth change and excitement in the students' hearts and lives, attacks would come from these pastors and even other missionaries. Sometimes pastors would even stand in their pulpits on Sundays and denounce the Bible school and discourage their members from attending. This happened quite frequently. But once again, what really surprised us was how much of the persecution came from Bible-believing churches. In reference to this opposition, we discovered what I refer to as three main areas of consciousness in pastors and ministers that cause these types of outbreaks of envy, jealousy, and competition. They are *man consciousness, money consciousness,* and *ministry* (position) *consciousness.*

Man consciousness: As Saul eyed David because of his success, so there are those who will measure themselves by others.

Money consciousness: At the root of this envy and jealousy is the fear that if people decide to leave the local church, they will take their money with them.

Ministry consciousness: This is the fear that if the people are more blessed by going to another church or ministry school, then the minister will lose his or her influence over them.

Can you see why these different pastors and ministers were threatened by the presence of these Bible training centers in their cities? Can you see how wrong their motives were? They were not interested in the people's spiritual well-being, but in their own well-being. This attitude should automatically disqualify an individual from ministry.

... "Woe to the shepherds of Israel who feed themselves! Should not the shepherds feed the flocks?" (Ezekiel 34:2)

Let's expose these three areas of consciousness that cause so many ministers and believers to operate out of their soul. First, let's talk about being man conscious.

Man Consciousness

For we dare not class ourselves or compare ourselves with those who commend themselves. But they, measuring themselves by themselves, and comparing themselves among themselves, are not wise (2 Corinthians 10:12).

In other words, if we are conscious of man, this is what will begin to happen. We'll begin to compare ourselves with others. The Bible says it is not wise to do so. When we start comparing ourselves with others, one of two things will begin to happen: either we will become puffed up with pride and feel superior, or we'll feel inadequate and inferior to them. Both of these reactions are wrong. When we compare ourselves with others, selfish ambition will take hold of our soul. We'll begin to desire to be more than what we are. No one can be more than what he or she is. We can only be what God has made us. That doesn't mean we cannot improve ourselves, grow, and develop in our walk and calling. It just means that our goal must not be a man, but Christ. If we're going to compare ourselves, then it must be against God's Word and against our own potential in Christ. As some have said, many of us struggle in who we would like to become instead of simply resting in who we are and who God has made us to be. The gifts, abilities, and callings of God on the inside of each of us are like seeds. A planted seed does not struggle to grow. The seed does not struggle to become something that it's not. If it's a corn seed, it doesn't struggle to be a carrot. It is what it is, and it rests in perfect contentment in the precise role God has purposed and equipped it to be. It is also patient during the different seasons it goes through. It is patient in those seasons until it begins to bear fruit.

But let patience have its perfect work, that you may be perfect and complete, lacking nothing (James 1:4).

The Lord said something to me one time early in ministry that really helped my thinking in this area. He said, "Until you are lacking in nothing, you will never be ready for something." Until we are complete in the season we are in, we are not ready for anything more. As long as we're struggling and striving to be something else, to be someone else, and to be somewhere else, then we are not ready for anything else. If we're struggling for a bigger name, a bigger church, or a bigger ministry, then we are not ready for it. We need to rest in who we are right now and let God bring the growth. The resting posture is what will actually loose God's hand to bring the increase and multiplication that He has ordained for our lives and ministries. However, we'll not get there if we continue walking and operating only out of our souls. If the seasons of God switch in our lives and we're not ready for the transition, then we won't make it. Why? Because we're in our souls.

How can we tell if we're operating out of our souls instead of our spirits? When we're anxious, frustrated, and eager to do something else we're in the soul and in the place where God cannot work and accelerate things in our lives and callings. But as we enter into rest and abide in it, we'll be able to move with God when the seasons change. To move with God we have to be in the Spirit. Being man conscious leads to selfish ambition, which denies access to the movement of divine activity in our lives. That's the main point here. Selfish ambition clouds the Spirit of God in our lives.

And do you seek great things for yourself? Do not seek them... (Jeremiah 45:5).

For all seek their own, not the things which are of Christ Jesus (Philippians 2:21).

Selfish ambition will drive us to do things that God never ordained for us to do. A greater divine focus in our lives and ministries will reverse this operation and result in a settling and a planting of our spirits deeper into the soil of our callings. Peter is a classic example of someone who had a very strong soul that was dispossessed from the Spirit of God. He possessed a lot of human ambition that needed tempering. He was very man conscious, and he had a great tendency to measure himself in the light of others.

Peter, seeing him, said to Jesus, "But Lord, what about this man?" (John 21:21)

Peter was inquiring of Jesus concerning John the Beloved. He wanted to know what would become of him. Jesus had just finished talking to Peter about his own life and calling and had commanded Peter to follow Him. While they're having this conversation, Peter turned around and saw John and began to ask about him. Peter's focus was completely off. Note Jesus' strong reply to Peter's misguided inquiry.

Jesus said to him, "If I want him to remain until I come, what is that to you? You follow Me!" (John 21:22 NAS)

In other words, Jesus told Peter that it was none of his business what would become of John. He stated emphatically the need for Peter to keep his eyes on Him and to follow Him. One of the greatest things that we can do in ministry is simply mind our own business and rejoice in our own work and labor in the Lord. Serve the Lord with gladness and singing and be content to have a part in His Kingdom. Let's be glad for all that God plans for us, and for what God is planning for others, even though it may be very different than His plans for us.

Money Consciousness

Then everyone left in your family line will come and bow down before him for a piece of silver and a crust of bread and plead, "Appoint me to some priestly office so I can have food to eat" (1 Samuel 2:36 NIV).

Our motive for ministry can never be money. Our motive for traveling and preaching the gospel cannot be to make a living. It can become very easy to choose where one goes by the financial offerings one will receive. Some ministers will naturally prefer the larger churches because they are generally more able to meet their budgets. However, God may have a different plan, and it's best to follow Him. Also, there are those who will use a relationship to gain access to finances and resources to help their own ministry.

For example, I remember when one of our young pastors in Africa came to a large conference in America many years ago. It was his first time in America, and his eyes got big. At this conference he was trying to meet different ministers in the hope of securing some resources for his church in Africa. Finally, one of the other missionaries managed to talk to him and straighten out his attitude. It's not wrong to want to meet different ministers, but this young pastor's motive for meeting them was totally off. Yes, relationships are very important, and many good things can come out of God-ordained relationships; however, we must watch our motives.

A prophet of God once said that many men in ministry have become money-minded and have thus lost the anointing. Some of them even died prematurely because of a wrong focus and wrong motives in ministry. This prophet gave an example of an evangelist who was mightily used of God back in the 1940's and 50's. This evangelist was conducting a big tent crusade, and on one of the nights, he called for five deaf and dumb people to come forward for ministry. Instantly, all five people were totally healed. It was a great display of God's miracle power. Immediately after this happened, the evangelist took up an offering. Of course, the people were far more generous with their giving after witnessing such an awesome deliverance. However, this man's motive was wrong. He was taking advantage of the opportunity to raise money. Sadly, this man was eventually judged and went home prematurely to be with the Lord at age 38. By his premature death, a tremendous ministry was taken away from the earth.

The unwholesome desire for money has caused many sorrows in the lives of many ministers. It has resulted in the compromise of men's integrity and brought a reproach to the gospel ministry and the name of Jesus. Money consciousness will cause ministers to do things that they otherwise would not do. Pressure tends to expose our hearts. This is why ministerial candidates need to be tested and proven before filling a ministry position of any great responsibility.

Let's look at the apostle Paul's attitude toward money:

What is my reward then? That when I preach the gospel, I may present the gospel of Christ without charge, that I may not abuse my authority in the gospel (1 Corinthians 9:18).

All things are lawful for me, but all things are not expedient: all things are lawful for me, but all things edify not (1 Corinthians 10:23 KJV).

Now for the third time I am ready to come to you. And I will not be burdensome to you; for I do not seek yours, but you. For the children ought not to lay up for the parents, but the parents for the children (2 Corinthians 12:14).

Paul is saying here that although he had the right and the privilege to receive offerings, he would not abuse that right. Even though Paul wrote that they who preach the gospel should live by the gospel (1 Cor. 9:14), he was also determined not to let this privilege hinder people from receiving the gospel and being blessed. Paul's first concern and priority was for the gospel to flow unhindered. When your priorities are properly aligned with the Lord's purposes, it's amazing how God will bless you even when men don't. I've been in situations when I felt cheated on an offering, but because I kept my heart right, God made it up to me somewhere down the road.

One time there was a pastor who was brought into a struggling church to replace another pastor. He quickly realized that part of the reason for the church's troubles was the people's lack of understanding and commitment to God's principles for finances. He purposed in his heart that he would begin to immediately teach on the subject of tithes and offerings. As he was preparing to do so, the Spirit of God began to witness to him that the time was not yet ripe for him to teach on the subject of finances. The people didn't know his heart yet, and so they did not have any confidence in him. The Lord instructed him that if he were to teach on tithing right away, half the people would leave the church. The pastor obeyed God and waited, and he was blessed because of it. Did that pastor have a right to teach on tithes and offerings? He most certainly did. However, doing so when he had first wanted to would have hindered the people from receiving the Word of God. A strong money-minded person would probably have foregone the witness of the Spirit and taught on finances anyway. However, he would have done a great disservice to those people and the gospel ministry.

When it comes to money and provision, it's much better to lean into the arena of the Spirit and put your total trust in God. Have the same attitude as Abraham, the father of faith.

But Abram said to the king of Sodom, "I have raised my hand to the Lord, God Most High, the Possessor of heaven and earth, that I will take nothing, from a thread to a sandal strap, and that I will not take anything that is yours, lest you should say, 'I have made Abram rich' " (Genesis 14:22-23).

Wow! Abraham knew who his source was and where his provision came from. Our attitude should be the same. Like Abraham, we should be able to say: "Lord, I am not going to try to make anything happen. If You are in this, then You will provide. I will look to neither man nor the arm of flesh for help. I make my vow to You, Lord God, to place my total trust in You." By making that declaration and consecration, you are acknowledging God as your God. If we don't trust Him completely with our finances, then He is not God in our lives.

Now let's move on to the last area of consciousness that produces soulish ministers instead of spiritual ones.

Ministry Consciousness

I wrote to the church, but Diotrephes, who loves to have the preeminence among them, does not receive us (3 John 9).

What we mean by ministry conscious is being position, rank, and authority minded. In the above verse John is warning the elder Gaius of this man Diotrephes. He had a bad attitude and was operating with a wrong spirit. He was power hungry and wanted to have the upper hand and rule in the church. Any man who reaches for authority is a potentially dangerous man. He will eventually create many problems for any church or ministry. We need leaders and people in our churches who are reaching for responsibility, not authority.

There is something about authority, influence, and power that can obsess a man. Men are conquerors and achievers by nature, and if they don't keep their egos sanctified, they can easily be deceived by false success. There are researchers today in the medical field who spend their entire lives looking for possible cures for terminal diseases. The competition is so great among them that they will actually withhold from sharing information with one another. Although they are all trying to save lives, each one is also striving for personal fame and notoriety. Each researcher wants to be that one who receives public praise and acclamation as the savior from a dreaded human disease, not to mention the unhindered and immeasurable cash flow that will be his throughout his entire life and the lives of his descendants. In ministry, it should be different, but oftentimes it's not. The same competition exists, as well as the same jostling for position and the same unwillingness to share ministry secrets with others because of the fear of a crowded market. Yet we, too, are trying to save the world!

Some men in a desperate quest to advance their ministries will bowl over anybody who may stand in their way. Being known is the name of the game. Marketing their own churches, their own ministries, and, of course, their own name, is top priority. Through positioning themselves for success and fame, all they birth is shame, shame, and more shame. They are position seekers whose ministries have become their mistresses.

That was Saul's problem. He was ministry conscious. He jealously and fiercely guarded his own popularity and influence. He murdered 85 of the Lord's priests and an entire city of men, women, and children because they had helped David. How many of the Lord's ministers do we kill with our mouths and attitudes? How many cities remain virtually untouched by the gospel because of all the competition and strife among ministers of that city?

Man consciousness, money consciousness, and ministry consciousness all contribute to a low-level soulish walk, which results in a low-level, low-impact life and ministry. When we operate strictly out of our souls, we will experience continual discontentment in our lives. God desires to bring us into a fulfillment of our callings and ministries, but it must be done His way. As I said before, we must pass through the different seasons. For instance, autumn is a season. It's a season of harvest. That's what we all want. But how many of us know that before autumn arrives, we must pass through summer? And before the summer, there is spring. And in order to see the spring, we must survive the winter. We can never jump straight from winter or spring to autumn. Perhaps God has shown you your autumn, your harvest, and the fullness of your calling, but you're still in the season of spring. You may have just been planted, or you may be just beginning to bud with bits of greenery. However, if you begin to grow frustrated and impatient in the particular season that you're in now, you'll miss God totally. This can happen very easily when we keep looking at the harvest in other men's lives and ministries. In other words, if we are man, money, or ministry conscious, we'll miss what God has for us. Those three areas are usually where we look for harvest. However, a farmer doesn't look for harvest during any other season except the harvest season.

If we only operate out of our soul or flesh, we'll stay in our winter season all the days of our lives. On the other hand, though, the more we walk in the Spirit, the shorter our seasons will be, and the quicker we'll get to harvest season. That's how it works.

In concluding this chapter, let me say one more thing. What really matters in all this is *the Lord's approval of our lives and ministries.*

..."*Let him who boasts boast in the Lord.*" *For it is not the one who commends himself who is approved, but the one whom the Lord commends* (2 Corinthians 10:17-18 NIV).

Whether men approve of you or not doesn't really matter. What counts is the Lord's approval of you. You can be unpopular with men and be consumed by the favor and approval of God. I think sometimes we assume that popularity with men means that we also have approval with God. More often than not, though, the very opposite is true. Some of the most unpopular men are men whom God's hand is really upon. The above Scripture tells us what the real test is. Is your boast in the Lord? Is He commending your life and ministry? Your response to those two questions will eventually determine your destiny.

Chapter 8

Human Government Versus Divine Government

...Give us a king... (1 Samuel 8:6).

...and the government will rest on His shoulders... (Isaiah 9:6 NAS).

So far in this book, I have referred to the kingdoms of Saul and David. I would now like to look closer at that which pertains to Saul (or what I will call human government) and compare it with that which is of David (or divine government). One type of government is man-made (Saul), while the other is ordered and established by God (David). Saul was chosen by the people, a king made by man. However, David was chosen and made by God. Saul was a soulish leader who operated out of selfish ambition and a jealous/competitive spirit. David was a spiritual leader who was unselfish and humble in spirit. The difference between these two types of leadership relates to the work that God has been doing in His Church for 2,000 years.

God has promised that there will be a separation and a distinction made between that which is wheat and that which is chaff. A sharper distinction shall be made between that which is born of God and that which is born of the flesh and of man. God wants His Church to walk in a greater measure of holiness and power. As she does, the distinction between the Church and the world will also be greater. Jesus is returning for a Bride who is holy and unblemished, and His Holy Spirit is getting us ready. Heaven is putting pressure on the Church of Jesus Christ to conform to His image. The fire and the heat will be turned up as we draw nearer to the coming of the King. Because leadership is most visible, this is where change will be most visible. God will purify His priests.

There are young "Davids" standing in the ranks who will come forth out of their present obscurity from among a sea of "Sauls" to build the Kingdom of God. They have been shepherds watching over another man's flock, and because of their faithfulness, they will be given that which is their own. These "Davids" will be qualified to reign because they've been prepared and trained. Righteous character has been formed, and holy foundations have been laid in them. Now God can build. God lays and builds. If you are not willing to lay low and stay low, God cannot build high. Let God lay you low so that He can build you high. Low-visibility, high-impact Christians are the only kind that God builds.

If you are going to be a "David," you're going to have to undergo the same sort of intensive training and preparation that he did. The key to becoming a spiritual leader, instead of a soulish one, lies in the type of training and preparation you receive. There are men who are trained of the letter and there are those who are "Spirit" trained. Many Bible schools and colleges in this land are humanistic in their training. They offer courses, doctrines, and ideologies that appeal to the soulish nature of man. They attract self-seeking and self-promoting people who are full of human ambition. It is a most dangerous thing to give authority and responsibility to such a man. It is dangerous to entrust such a person with the lives of other people. Do you know why? Because their motives, which are the bedrock of godly character, are tainted and polluted with selfish ambition. If a man's motives are wrong, his methods will be as well. If a man's foundation is not laid right, he will not build right. Foundations are what give strength to a structure. There are all kinds of spiritual structures that were not designed by the Master Builder. These structures are not safe, but dangerous. When they crumble and fall, many people will be hurt, and there may even be some who will never recover.

"Their Might Is Not Right"

That which is of human government or of "Saul" will not stand on that day for the fire of God will consume it. Fire consumes wood, hay, and stubble, which represents our own plans and self-seeking motives and methods. Saul used questionable and corrupt means to secure his own personal success. He used his power and position unjustly, but God deals very strongly with leaders who abuse their authority. (Read Jeremiah 23 and Matthew 23.) We know that the men whom Jesus rebuked were the religious leaders of that day. We may also remember how sternly God dealt with Moses when he struck the rock twice. Many other examples could be listed from the Scriptures. We must be careful how we build our lives and ministries. To whom much is given, much is required (Lk. 12:48). Leaders shall receive a more severe judgment and stricter condemnation (Jas. 3:1).

...their might is not right (Jeremiah 23:10 NAS).

Like the disciples of Jesus who were expecting the Lord to set up His earthly throne in Jerusalem, there are many today with the same mindset. Again, like the disciples, these leaders will try to go so far as to call down fire from Heaven against anyone who will get in the way of them setting up an earthly kingdom to rule. They will protect what they feel is their "own" territory when others seek to "trespass" therein. When a new church or a new ministry moves into their particular city or town, these soulish leaders feel threatened and immediately begin to discredit the newcomers in the name of being "spiritual" watchmen. In reality, though, they are not at all interested in the name and fame of Jesus being voiced abroad, only their own name and fame. These leaders display a spirit that tears down and destroys instead of builds up and saves. Furthermore, the disciples were more concerned about people belonging to their particular ministry team than the fact that these people were doing the works of Jesus (see Lk. 9:49). Would you agree that in 2,000 years very little has changed in this regard? As a matter of fact, it seems to have gotten worse. We ought to rejoice when people get blessed, no matter who the blessing is coming through. That's why Jesus kept drilling the disciples that the greatest in the Kingdom of God is the one who serves. Our qualification to lead is based upon our willingness to serve. This is probably the number one Kingdom principle, especially concerning leadership.

Again, there are leaders who are considered great by earthly measure and earthly terms, but who are not known by Heaven (Mt. 7:21-23). They appear to be very successful and prominent leaders on the earth, but the Lord Jesus doesn't know them. They may speak and prophesy in His name, but it's really in their own name. They may cast out demons and do wonderful works in Jesus' name, but it's their own name they are interested in promoting. Oh, what a fearful day it will be when that which was said and done in the secret places of our hearts will be revealed!

That which is of the order of human government pursues a human kingdom, while that which is of divine government pursues the divine One. They are after God. Human government, or that which pertains to "Saul," will multiply to himself horses, wives, silver, and gold (Deut. 17:16-17). In other words, he will use whatever resources are at his disposal to make a name and kingdom for himself. Saul used the people and their gifts and resources to serve him and his kingdom. Whenever he found anyone with particular skills and talents, he recruited them (1 Sam. 14:52). A leader's purpose is to serve the people. The people are not merely gifts to serve the leader. Actually, the proper perspective is that the minister and the people he leads are to serve the heavenly vision that God has ordained together. Everyone should serve one another as unto the Lord. That's the way it's supposed to work.

As we have already seen, Saul's position and achievements became his idol, and he protected his own kingdom and name with vicious animosity. Saul possessed an "ownership" mentality over a kingdom and a people that were not his; they belonged to God. That's when a controlling and competitive evil spirit began to dominate him. Again, this is a spirit that is very prevalent in ministry today. A soulish leader will use any means to gain and to keep people when they are viewed only as resources for accomplishing his vision and goals. In this particular form of human government, compromise will rule. Sin will go unchecked. The leaven of Egypt or the world will become very influential.

Leaders of human government seek earthly honor and approval and will do almost anything to get it and keep it. They will not rebuke sin or its festering leaven from among the people because of a fear that they might leave. Ironically, the people are the ones who support the programs that uphold the leader's vision and ministry. Saul was commanded to utterly destroy the Amalekites and all their possessions (1 Sam. 15:1-3), but he did not do so because he feared the people (1 Sam. 15:15,21,24). When the prophet Samuel called Saul to give account for his actions, he confessed his sin, but he did not forsake the root cause and hideous sin of loving the honor of men more than the honor of God (1 Sam. 15:30). Under pressure, Saul's love for popularity, publicity, and the approval of men proved greater than his love for God and his hatred of sin. Saul feared man and the inevitable persecution that comes from pure obedience to the Lord. He wanted acceptance from the people, but instead, he received rejection from God (1 Sam. 15:26). In attempting to embrace and possess a kingdom for himself, Saul lost the kingdom. Saul spent the rest of his days protecting his personal interests in the Kingdom—at David's expense. Actually, Saul spent more time scheming to kill and destroy David than he did anything else. This again affirms the truth of all ages: There will always be war between that which pertains to human government and that which pertains to divine government. The *good news* is that divine government will grow increasingly stronger as we near the end of this age, while human government will wax weaker and weaker (2 Sam. 3:1). The *best news* is that of the increase "of His [divine] government and peace there shall be no end..." (Is. 9:7 KJV). May we be delivered from our "Sauls" and found among His government.

Chapter 9

Characteristics
of Divine Government

While Saul was using his power unjustly, David loomed in the shadows, and in the sunlight of God's providence and favor, he was being prepared to take Saul's place. There is a remnant, a new breed that God preserves for Himself in every generation. David represents that form of divine government. The following is a part of a prophetic utterance concerning the training and preparation of these "Davids."

"For a new breed of troops to arise there must be given a new breed of training. For many of My past trainees have only been trained for the easy and the soft, not for the rigorous and the hard. Many have been trained of the letter but not of the Spirit, and so they stand unequipped for battle and as easy targets for the enemy. Sow to the Spirit and so shall their swords be sharpened, for the flesh has made them dull. For in the flesh is weariness and hands that let the shield of faith hang down. Prepare My troops to march to a different spirit. Root out the flesh, selfish ambition, and pride, and train them to walk by My side, for I resist the proud but give grace to the humble."

David possessed the godly characteristics that every leader should have because of the training and preparation he yielded himself to. First of all, the godly traits birthed in him were a result of David's willingness to remain in obscurity and in a "wilderness" place of training. Second, they were birthed in him because he allowed himself to be broken by the fiery tests and trials that he endured. Very little of God can be birthed in an unbroken vessel. I've heard it said that the greatest fruit in our own lives and ministries will come forth from that which we have gained through application, experience, and suffering.

David was anointed to be king while he was yet a teenager. And it was as a teenager that he fought and won his great victory against Goliath, but it wasn't until many years later, at the age of 30, when he began to reign. There is a divine training, preparation, and order to the formation of a godly leader and ministry. There must be a period of withdrawal and seclusion before public service and ministry. The sword must be administered to our own souls so that nothing of our natural lives will influence or stand in the way of God's purpose. The ministration of Christ can never fully come forth from us until then. Our souls will continue to rule us until we're sharpened by the Spirit. There are far too many hirelings and too few shepherds in leadership today. There are far too many leaders who rule and lead by their souls. Yet, there are many "Joshuas" waiting for their "Moses"; and many "Timothys" looking for their "Paul." We have many spiritual sons who are without spiritual fathers, and so they've learned to make the presence of their heavenly Father their portion. David was such a one.

Saul possessed an itch for popularity and publicity; but to David, publicity was a burden, and the honor of God was his foremost desire. Saul feared man, but David feared God. While Saul pursued a position and protected his power and popularity, David was engrossed in pursuing God. What a difference there is between these two types of leadership. David's focus caused him to increase in divine character and authority, while Saul merely increased in the operation of soulish manipulation and human planning. David was learning to walk in more and more humility and brokenness, but Saul walked continually in pride and jealousy. Keeping his kingdom and receiving credit for his achievements was Saul's sole (soul) quest. David, however, was willing to release the kingdom to Absalom only to have God return it to him later.

A "David" Trusts God

David knew that no man or kingdom (ministry or organization) could control his calling and destiny. God and David alone controlled it: It was God's work and plan and David's submission to that plan that brought his success. No man can bring you where you are going; only God can do it. He'll move mountains if necessary, if you will only cooperate with Him and walk in the Spirit. Listen and respect leaders, but follow the Lord.

David did not attempt to protect his ministry and calling from others. He knew that God could keep what God had given him. David was not in competition with anyone. He had nothing to prove and no bones to pick with anybody. How different that attitude is from so many modern ministries and churches today who call themselves by Christ's name. How many leaders are releasing authority in their churches and ministries to others today? How many of the "big" guys are helping the "little" guys in ministry? How many missionaries are planting new works and releasing full authority of them to national leadership? It is a lot easier said than done.

My wife and I had the privilege of serving nine years as missionaries in three different countries in West Africa. During this time we served under another man's vision (a God-given vision) and ministry. During our last three years, God helped us to pioneer and establish a work in one of these West African Islamic countries, but the Lord told us to completely release it to national leadership. By the grace of God, we managed to build up the work to a place where we were just doing leadership and missionary training. It started to become real enjoyable. In the natural, we were as comfortable as we had ever been on the mission field, and things were quite cozy. To be perfectly truthful about it, in my soul I really did not want to relinquish full authority of that work to national leadership, but the Lord was leading us to do it. We had invested tens of thousands of dollars into this work and built up a nice base of operations to launch out further into Africa, or perhaps even start our own missionary organization. However, this was not God's plan for us. I tried to talk the Lord into at least keeping some oversight of it, but He wouldn't let me do it. "Release it all, return to the States, and start a new ministry," He said. That was scary!

"But Lord," I reasoned, "this is our vineyard, and these people are our fruit. We have a right to eat of this vineyard. We raised the money to purchase all this sound and office equipment and supplies. It was our money that was used to ship all this stuff over here. Besides, Lord, who is going to support us now that we are not full-fledged missionaries?" Can you see how the ownership mentality had begun to set in? This is the mindset behind human government. It was not an easy decision to let it all go, and although we lost about one third of our support in the transition process, the Lord has blessed us in many other ways.

The fire of God comes to separate that which is of man from that which is of God. Fire consumes wood, hay, and straw, but refines gold, silver, and precious stones (1 Cor. 3:10-13). Again, wood, hay, and straw represent our own plans, motives, and methods, which are based on the love of self. Saul's kingly ministry was based on love of self. Although he started out as a humble man, through increase of the kingdom, he became proud, jealous, and competitive. However, the foundation of David's kingly rule and ministry was based on the love that he possessed for God and for the people.

> *Therefore Saul removed him from his presence, and made him his captain over a thousand; and he [David] went out and came in before the people. ... But all Israel and Judah loved David, because he went out and came in before them* (1 Samuel 18:13,16).

A "Saul" Loves Himself

David loved the people, and the people loved him. Apparently he led Saul's men out to battle. He was a shepherd to them and was highly esteemed by them. Read First Chronicles 12 and note the number of men who followed David's leadership. He earned their trust to such an extent that some even risked their lives by crossing through enemy lines just to fetch David a drink of water (1 Chron. 11:17-19). On the other hand, Saul appeared oppressive in his leadership of Israel. At one point when the Philistines were mounting their forces against Israel, Saul's men became distressed and trembled as they followed him. Some of the troops went into hiding, and others eventually became scattered from him (1 Sam. 13:5-8). They had no confidence in Saul and not much loyalty to him either. I wonder why?

In another instance, Saul's men again became distressed because Saul had pronounced a curse over anyone who ate any food before the evening (1 Sam. 14:24). He bound the people under an oath. That is what oppressive leadership does. It binds people with unreasonable demands instead of setting them free. It doesn't appear that Saul moved in and out among the people like David did. He did not have a shepherd's heart. Conversely, David possessed a great shepherd's heart, and everyone was drawn to the safety and security of his compassion. It does not seem that David ever had to recruit men as Saul did (see 1 Sam. 14:52), but the Lord sent multitudes of men to help David in his kingship and in building the kingdom. He also remembered his friends, the elders, and those who stayed by the stuff at home (what we would call the ministry of helps today). David sent them all gifts and shared the spoils of war with them (1 Sam. 30:24-26).

Leaders need to remember those who contributed to their success in ministry. This is one of the ways in which a leader can show a genuine gratitude and appreciation for others. It is also a key way in which the people gain a love and respect for the leader. This is very important. I knew of a pastor who was prospering financially in his life and ministry while one of his associate families who had helped him and his family succeed was struggling greatly. Due to a lack of appreciation and willingness on the senior pastor's part to help his struggling associate, a family was hurt and wounded. This eventually led to a bitter separation between two good families. My wife and I have been on both sides of this issue ourselves. Sometimes we have been left wishing that we had been more sensitive to those who have helped us in our life and ministry, and at other times, we have felt as if we were not allowed to be partakers or sharers of blessings we had helped to create. If a leader is living in near luxury and he has associates living in near poverty, he has a responsibility to help them, especially if they have helped him get to where he is today.

This genuine love and concern for the people, such as David possessed, is another key feature that marks us as belonging to the rule and reign of divine government. Everything that our Lord Jesus Christ ever did was for the people. Jesus was not called the great preacher or the great teacher, but the Great Shepherd (Heb. 13:20) because of His genuine love for the people. Jesus went out among the masses and spent precious time with individuals as well. He cared for their needs. Such are those leaders who pertain to "David." These leaders are unselfish. Their might is right; they use their power justly.

Oh God, give us more "Davids"!

Chapter 10

Soulish Vision

Many people in the Body of Christ today have their own ministry, but they were never called by God to be a leader of a ministry. They never had a dream, a vision, a divine mandate, or a word from the Lord on it. They have unsanctified ambition that has moved them to invent a vision. They are products of soulish and carnal teaching on success in ministry. They worship success and not the Lord Jesus Christ. They are in the wrong place and are carrying a wrong vision. Some have even been moved by seeing genuine needs and sincerely desiring to help meet those needs. However, seeing a need does not constitute a call. Jesus saw many needs that He never did anything about. He only did what the Father asked Him to do.

Then there are those who have been hurt and wounded in ministry. As a result, they are offended, brokenhearted, distraught, and confused. They may be malfunctioning in their gift and calling or not functioning at all. Some Saul-like leaders are to blame for their hurt. Now paralyzed by the negative emotions flowing from their soul, their vision has become obscured by a satanic onslaught. Their hurt caused them to lose their desire for the things of God, and they have no responsive chords in their heart that still ring for the Lord or for ministry. Some even have a high calling and a vision from the Lord, but due to their hurt, they can only operate from the soul.

Finally, there is a third group (which has already been addressed in this book in part). These are persons who may be called and have received a vision or word from the Lord, but they are operating with a wrong spirit, bringing damage to the Body of Christ and themselves. They are among the multitude of "Sauls" who have wrong motives for ministry. They are soulish leaders who may have had spiritual vision at one time, but have now lost it. Some may even be sincere and want to serve God but are greatly deceived.

These three categories of people have what I call "soulish vision." Soulish vision is that which is either birthed or carried in our souls. Our souls are made up of the will, intellect, and emotions. Our souls are on a lower level than our spirits, which is the part of us that communes with God. Spiritual vision comes from the heart of God and is birthed in our heart out of our fellowship with God, whereas soulish vision is birthed by our thought processes and imagination apart from the influence of the Spirit of God.

Wait on God

Spiritual vision comes from our willingness to worship the Lord and wait on Him for wisdom, guidance, and direction. Soulish vision, however, comes as a result of our unwillingness to worship the Lord and be in patient waiting for His will, plan, and direction to be revealed. Remember, that was the initial reason why Saul was rejected by the Lord and the kingdom torn from him; he was impatient in waiting for Samuel to minister in the priestly office during a time of war. Saul's impatience under pressure cost him the kingdom. Our impatience can cost us our very lives and ministries as well.

> *Go down ahead of me to Gilgal. I will surely come down to you to sacrifice burnt offerings and fellowship offerings, but you must **wait** seven days until I come to you and tell you what you are to do* (1 Samuel 10:8 NIV).

Saul was instructed by Samuel to wait for him so that he could make offering and sacrifice to the Lord and show Saul what he should do. But the pressure was mounting from the enemy, and the people were fearful, in distress, and hiding or becoming scattered from Saul (1 Sam. 13:5-12). So what was Saul's great sin? Saul missed it primarily in two areas: *timing* and *anointing*. First, it was the wrong time: He failed to wait for Samuel and the word of the Lord. Second, it was the wrong anointing. Saul usurped the priestly office. He was a king, but he attempted to administer the ordinances of a priest. Saul did what many of us have done. He reacted to pressure and allowed that pressure to pull him out of God's timing and anointing.

If we're not careful, we will allow such a drive for success to build up inside of us that we will forge ahead with any plan that seems good and force it to happen (see 1 Sam. 13:12). Most of the time our choices in this area are not even made out of a genuine love for the people, but out of a desire to just be successful. We're either trying to draw a bigger crowd or trying to appease the people into staying with us. In an attempt to gain the success and ministry results of their peers, leaders will sometimes copy or imitate their ideas, programs, ministry styles, and strategies. We can pattern after principles, but we must all seek our strategies from the

Lord. At other times, leaders can try to just do it all and fail to recognize the different anointings, assignments, emphases, and visions that God disperses to the Body of Christ. Again, they may even have the right vision for their lives and ministry, but it can become clouded by their own thinking and reasoning. All these ingredients work to create what I call soulish vision.

Abraham received a word from the Lord concerning the birth of Isaac. He had the right vision, but he missed the timing and tried to force it to happen. Isn't it amazing how we are always trying to help God bring His word to pass? Abraham's soulish planning and reasoning gave birth to soulish vision, and it all happened because of impatience.

Many times when we check our hearts we may find that we are doing things for the wrong reasons. We want to enhance our reputations and appear successful to the public eye. What was it that Saul feared most in the situation with the Philistines? He was afraid of failure and defeat and the ruin of his reputation. Likewise, fear of failure often motivates us to act prematurely and irrationally.

Ingredients for Failure

Impatience is not the only ingredient that contributes to soulish vision; pride is another one. Pride makes us do things for the wrong reasons. (We will look at the subject of pride more closely in the next chapter.) We often act in certain ways in order to protect ourselves from failure and to look good in the eyes of others. Sometimes all our talk about excellence in ministry is nothing but an outward show that is used to cover up our own spiritual deficiencies. The spirit of excellence that Daniel possessed did not have its roots in outward appearance (Dan. 6:3). It involved seeing, perceiving, understanding, and interpreting the will and plan of God. Daniel's spirit of excellence was spiritual vision. It is certainly honorable to have things look nice, but let's not pass it off as a spirit of excellence. There are brethren in Africa, India, and China who don't have the means to adorn outward temples, but who have a far greater spirit of excellence than we do.

The fact is, in America the two ingredients listed above—impatience and pride—are two of the biggest problems in our nation. They are also two of the biggest problems in our churches, especially among leaders. They are the primary reasons why there has been so much soulish, shallow, and superficial Christianity in America. Let us not do foolishly as Saul did, but rather, let's each be found to have a heart after God (1 Sam. 13:13-14).

Oh God, give us more men with spiritual vision.

Chapter 11

Pride

God resists the proud, and the proud resist God. God is heavenly and from above. Pride is hellish and from below. That fact alone should make us want to hate pride with a fury and a passion. Soulish and carnal leaders yield to pride, but spiritual leaders resist it.

Pride is a thief and a robber of man's spiritual destiny. It offers men earthly fruit in exchange for paradise, earthly profit in exchange for their souls, and the smile and earthly approval of men in exchange for the approval of God. Pride gives birth to idolatry and hypocrisy. It kills revival and the unity of the Spirit. When there is no unity of the Spirit, especially among leadership, there will be very little blessing (Ps. 133).

I remember a minister sharing a vision he had years ago about a man who was tending a very large field. The field was an endless pasture that represented the world. This man was laboring in this field by himself. Nobody was helping him. The reason why nobody was helping him was because of the vain imaginations and lies that others believed about him. The reason why this man wasn't working with others was because of the vain imaginations and lies he believed concerning them. Pride keeps leaders from approaching one another and communicating with each other openly and from the heart. Pride keeps leaders from networking together and sharing their abilities and resources. The harvest fields of this world are far too great for any one man, church, or ministerial organization to labor alone. Granted, leaders do not all have the same vision and purpose, but we certainly need one another, and we ought to be able to help each other. Ministers also have different functions, specializations, and ranks. By rank, I am referring to the different levels of authority in ministry. Pride causes us to try to be equal with men who have a higher rank, authority, and influence than ourselves. It may also cause peers of the same rank and authority to compete and try to outdo and outsucceed each other.

If we cannot rejoice in another minister's success, then we have a problem. Many ministers are for you until they feel (in their own minds, anyway), that you're outsucceeding them. (Of course, there's no such thing as outsucceeding a brother or sister in Christ, for success is simply obedience to what God is telling you to do.) We must guard against the constant temptation to compare and compete with anyone. This is what causes much of the strife and the grudges between ministers and leaders, and it has become a huge problem in the Body of Christ among ministers at all levels of authority. This is why there are churches and ministries everywhere that God never ordained. It is also why churches and pastors won't even announce and encourage people to attend special meetings by reputable and credible ministries in their city. Some pastors just can't lay down their own agenda and desires for even a day to join in helping and supporting another. Ultimately the people are the ones who suffer most and miss out on special blessings because of the childish attitudes of their leadership.

When we were in Africa as missionaries, we witnessed such a high degree of strife, jealousy, and competition among leaders—missionaries with other missionaries, churches with churches, missionaries with churches. It was so pathetic. They were like private armies fighting a civil war. How all this must grieve the Commander in Chief of this army and His Holy Spirit of unity! Any normal, national army recognizes and submits to rank, order, and authority and will work together for a common cause. Why can't the greatest army on this earth, the Church of Jesus Christ, do the same? May God help us.

Types of Pride

Pride among leaders primarily manifests in five different areas—positional pride, organizational pride, doctrinal pride, nationalistic pride, and spiritual pride. These five areas are responsible for the lack of unity in the Body of Christ. We are not speaking of a man-made unity that is wrought by the strength of human hands, but a true spiritual unity that is wrought by the Spirit of God. A false unity is one of conformity, but a spiritual unity is one of diversity. Leaders all have different functions, graces, visions, callings, mandates, and assignments from the Lord. Each one has a different rank or degree of authority. We need to respect those differences, but we must also realize that we can still have unity in our diversity. For instance, the parts of our physical body are all diverse in their operation, but they are also in unity, aren't they? (See First Corinthians 12:12-27.) Your hand and foot work differently and separately, but when your foot itches, your hand will stoop down (humility) to scratch it.

Furthermore, your whole body must cooperate when you are taking a shower in the morning, getting dressed, or successfully performing most other tasks.

Jesus has given His entire Body the task of evangelizing and discipling the world. Why is it taking so long? It is because the members of this body are not all cooperating. When the "foot" of Christ's Body itches and asks the "hand" for help in scratching it, the hand often replies, "Help yourself. Believe God like I do! I'm too busy anyway." As a result, the Body of Christ is so fragmented and divided in the different towns, cities, and regions of the world.

A closer look at the five primary areas of pride should help us to better understand this fragmentation.

Positional Pride

Miriam and Aaron desired to be equals in authority with Moses (Num. 12:2). In Numbers 16, we find that Korah and 250 princes of the assembly of Israel desired the same. They even accused Moses of being proud (Num. 16:3), but the truth was that pride was the beam that was stuck in their own eye (see Mt. 7:1-5). These men who rose up against Moses were leaders and ministers themselves, but they were not of the same rank and authority as Moses. No gift can be exalted above authority. Rather, every gift is to be *subject* to authority.

Jesus warned His disciples against the love of position and titles (Mt. 23:8-10). The basic reason for all the persecution in Jesus' day and in the early days of the Church was because the chief priests and Pharisees were losing authority and influence over the people (Jn. 11:47-48; Acts 13:44-45).

Their position was being threatened. Missionaries will put down other missionaries for the same reasons. Traveling ministers and pastors will do the same as well. But the reverse can also be true. Many times, persons with gifts and ministries of greater authority and power will not take time to help those who are lesser. They will withhold revelatory information from them because they don't want these smaller ministries to become as influential as they are, and it is due to positional pride. God's remedy for this type of pride is found in Matthew 23:11-12. It's when we humble ourselves that we truly qualify to serve in positions of authority.

Organizational Pride

The Jews said, in effect, to the former blind man who was now healed: "You are Jesus' disciple, but we belong to Moses. Our leader heard God, but we don't know about your leader" (see Jn. 9:28-29). The Corinthians said the same type of thing: "We belong to Paul. We are of Apollos' group. He's a better speaker. We follow Peter. He's the rock" (1 Cor. 1:12; 3:3-4). Now it is normal for spiritual babies or new converts to act this way, but today we have leaders displaying similar behavior. Their attitude is: "Our church is the best church. We have the most talented musicians and greatest choir. We have the finest organization. Our buildings and facilities are the most beautiful. This ministry is reaching more people than anyone." They may even say something like this: "We belong to this movement [or this camp or this denomination]. Our spiritual father and leader is so and so, and we follow him." What if your movement or camp or spiritual father gets off track? What will you do then? Will you follow that person or group into the ditch or over the cliff?

We may not voice these things out loud, but in our hearts we are really proud to be "Pentecostal," "Charismatic," "Word of Faith," or "Evangelical." We are proud to label ourselves as "Full Gospel" or "New Testament" or "Holiness" people. Perhaps we're more proud to identify ourselves as being more "traditional" or "conservative" or "fundamental." Perhaps you are proud to be a disciple of some famous personality, prestigious seminary, or popular Bible college. How much more can you become subject to these attitudes if you are the founder, pastor, or president of an organization. God doesn't care about names, labels, and organizations; He cares about people. Jesus didn't die for any organization; He died for human beings. It's only when leaders have been delivered of organizational pride that they are actually fit to run one.

Doctrinal Pride

The Pharisees' interpretation of the law claimed that a man could not labor or be healed on the Sabbath (Mk. 2:23-24; 3:2). They argued and fussed about such things as divorce (Mt. 19:3), associating with sinners (Mt. 9:11), and fasting (Mt. 9:14). They were teachers and experts of the law, but they failed to recognize the Lawgiver. They were near the Light, but pride blocked their sight. They worshiped a doctrinal god that didn't care about people.

Your doctrine may be right but your emphasis may be wrong. You may be right in your methods but wrong in your motives. You may be right in your form but lacking in your faith. You may be full of knowledge but empty of love. The All-Knowing One sees your emptiness and your pride; you cannot hide anything from Him.

Pride keeps us bound to wrong doctrine. Pride also makes us boast of right doctrine. Doctrine is important, but many times, it keeps leaders from joining arms and laboring together. If we would clothe ourselves with humility and a teachable spirit, God would give us the Holy Spirit to lead us and guide us into all truth. We are not fit to be teachers of doctrine until we are free of doctrinal pride.

Nationalistic Pride

The woman at the well challenged Jesus with her racial remarks (Jn. 4:9). The Samaritans would not receive Jesus because He was going to Jerusalem to be with the Jews (Lk. 9:51-53). In the midst of a move of God, racial undercurrents threatened to drown the unity of the early Church (Acts 6:1). Even the apostle Peter refrained from eating with the Gentiles when Jewish believers showed up, and Barnabas and other Jewish Christians joined in the hypocrisy until they were rebuked by Paul (Gal. 2:11-13).

Nationalistic pride has always been a problem in the Church; it has resulted in conflicts of race against race, ethnic group against ethnic group, and nationality against nationality. Satan has managed to breed a strong antichrist spirit of hatred and prejudice within the ranks of the Church. Christ prayed that we would be one (see Jn. 17). Christ bled and died to make us one. Christ sent the Holy Spirit into our hearts so that we could all cry, "Abba Father!" (Gal. 4:6) We are all brethren in the same family with the same Father. In Christ there is neither Jew nor Greek, male nor female (Gal. 3:28). We have to be careful about putting an emphasis on being a certain color, nationality, culture, tribe, or gender. There has been a strong women's movement that has bred a spirit of arrogance, independence, and rebellion among some women of the Church. We are called to lift people up in who they are in Christ, but we must lift them up in the spirit, not in the soul, the natural part of man. A proper attitude toward the gifts and roles of others will result in freedom and unity across the Body. We are called to make disciples of Jesus Christ, not of any particular race or nationality. That's nothing short of a Nazi spirit at work. Hitler attempted to make the whole world disciples of the German race. One of the greatest challenges almost every missionary faces is breaking down these barriers of culture, race, and nationality. It's one of the reasons why many missionaries are never received by the people they are sent to; the so-called "national" church rejects them. When we first went to Africa as missionaries, one of the local African ministers told us that Africa didn't need any more white missionaries. "Just give us the finances and the tools we need to do the job," he said. This is the mentality of many "nationals" because some foreign missionaries with a superiority complex have hurt them at some point. What does God think about all this? How does He see it? God sees us according to grace, not race; function, not faction; and calling, not color. God is color-blind.

This nationalistic spirit is one that totally devalues and demeans the blood of Jesus, and it grieves the Holy Spirit. Until our leaders nail this ugly spirit to the cross of their own lives, it will continue to dethrone the cause for which Jesus suffered and died.

Spiritual Pride

One of Jesus' disciples forbade someone from operating in the deliverance ministry because he didn't belong to the group that traveled with Jesus (Lk. 9:49-50). Organizational pride was working here, but so was spiritual pride. Spiritual pride happens in the Body of Christ when we oppose others because they aren't doing what we are doing in ministry or because they are not going where we are going. We become puffed up in our own vision and function and esteem it greater than any other.

Spiritual pride is probably the most subtle of all. This may be for those who are reading this book right now and thinking about all the leaders they know who need to read this. You may be reading this book and saying, "Amen! Too many leaders are soulish and full of pride. They need to hear this." But you may be the one in pride.

No two churches, ministries, or gifts are exactly alike. No two callings or visions are exactly the same. There may be similarities between them, but there are differences, too. Why aren't leaders more discerning and appreciative of these differences? Why is there so much misunderstanding between the fivefold ministry gifts? Why is there so much self-promotion at the expense of demoting others? What is it within you that wants to contribute to another's downfall?

Why do big and small ministries sometimes despise each other? Why does the "little guy" who has character and a good heart always get slighted by the "big guy" who has all the money and notoriety but sometimes lacks character? Why is there so little of the spirit of Him who "made Himself of no reputation, and took upon Him the form of a servant" in our leadership and ministries (Phil. 2:7 KJV)?

We can sometimes be partial and favor those ministers whom we like or who are most like us, while being critical or less accepting of those who aren't. However, it is those who are not like us whom we may need the most. We need every part and member of the Body of Christ, but spiritual pride will turn every man aside and make him a legend in his own mind.

Resisting Pride

*When you come to the land which the Lord your God is giving you, and possess it and dwell in it, and say, "I will set a king over me like all the nations that are around me," you shall surely set a king over you whom the Lord your God chooses; one from among your brethren you shall set as king over you; you may not set a **foreigner** over you, who is not your brother. But he shall not multiply **horses for himself**, nor cause the people to return to Egypt to multiply horses, for the Lord has said to you, "You shall not return that way again." Neither shall he multiply **wives for himself**, lest his heart turn away; nor shall he greatly multiply **silver and gold for himself**. Also it shall be, when he sits on the throne of his kingdom, that he shall write for himself a **copy of this law** in a book, from the one before the priests, the Levites. And it shall be with him, and he shall read it all the days of his life, that he may learn to fear the Lord his God and be careful to observe all the words of this law and these statutes, that **his heart may not be lifted above his brethren**, that he may not turn aside from the commandment to the right hand or to the left, and that he may prolong his days in his kingdom, he and his children in the midst of Israel* (Deuteronomy 17:14-20).

These verses explain the law of the administration of the king. I believe this law applies to every leader today. These instructions from God's Word are critical. They are great medicine and are guaranteed to keep leaders out of the intensive care unit of leadership. If someone like king Saul had hearkened to these instructions, he would not have missed God. This law is a warning against pride and tells us how to avoid pride and walk in humility.

Let's look at these verses. The first thing that God says here is that man shall not choose or appoint a leader, but that God Himself would appoint a leader of His choice. Here again, we see the importance of divine government versus human government. The selection of a wrong leader can cause so many problems. Leaders in God's Kingdom must be brethren, not foreigners (Deut. 17:15). On the surface, this seems to obviously indicate that we should not select an unbeliever to lead, but the implication here is much stronger than that. It is also saying that a leader must have a right spirit, the spirit of a true brother, not a foreign or a strange spirit. Spirits are transferable, especially from leaders.

Second, God does not want His Church and His leaders to govern themselves according to the way of Egypt or the world. There are several admonitions in these verses, and one of them is for leaders not to strengthen themselves with the strength of Egypt (the arm of flesh). Leaders are also not to add increase to themselves (Deut. 17:16-17). Why? The pursuit of personal increase will cause their hearts to turn away from fully following the Lord. When a leader begins to accumulate increase for himself, it becomes easier for him to esteem himself higher than he ought to. It also becomes a great temptation for him to compromise his integrity and use questionable means to maintain that increase.

There are three major things that have contributed to the downfall of almost every leader throughout the generations: the *glory*, the *girls*, and the *gold*. These three things are exactly what God warns Israel and its leaders against in these verses. Deuteronomy 17:17 speaks of the girls and the gold. Verse 16 speaks of horses, which would add to the strength and glory of the king. Sadly, these three areas have brought down many modern-day ministers and preachers. Any one of us can fall if we fail to take the strong preventive medicine that God offers in His Word.

Finally, God tells us that the reading, keeping, and doing of His Word is what will teach every leader the fear of the Lord and keep him from pride and from turning aside from God's purpose. Obedience in these things also carries the promise of life and longevity for the leader, his family, and ministry (Deut. 17:18-20). Let's keep God's purpose and ways always before us.

Chapter 12

Spiritual Vision

That which is born of the flesh is flesh, and that which is born of the Spirit is spirit (John 3:6).

But we will give ourselves continually to prayer and to the ministry of the word (Acts 6:4).

The Spirit is to the Church what blood is to the physical body. When popular concepts of church leadership center more on executive business principles than on the Word of God, the church will become soulish. When the focus of our ministry and preaching is to appeal to the soulish nature of man, then we will attract and produce those types of people. This will result in a church becoming large but lifeless. No matter how professional or elaborate the church is, how great the organization may be, or how large the attendance; if the Spirit of God is not working, all is in vain. Is the Lord building the house or is man (Ps. 127:1)?

Spiritual or Superficial?

Leaders can talk about "big" vision, getting people excited and making a lot of noise, but is it spiritual? Or, is it merely superficial? That's the criteria for judging what is really happening. It's easy to get people excited about personal wealth, prosperity, and success, but it's not so easy to get them excited about fasting and praying and winning souls. Spiritual vision is souls. If you've lost the burden for souls you've lost your vision. If you've lost your passion for the city and area that you're called to, then you need to ask the Lord to help you recover it. When leaders lose their burden for souls, the Holy Spirit begins to lose His influence. Time in prayer and in the Word is necessary to restore the burden of the Lord to a ministry. Intimacy with Jesus restores broken focus and gives birth to spiritual vision. This is the way to create space for the Holy Spirit to have precedence. Give the Spirit space so that the Lord Jesus will have preeminence. In this way, it will be the Lord who builds the church, not you.

Where there is lack of emphasis on reaching the lost and the people are without a burden for them, the following thing will begin to happen. First, people will develop a form of godliness that lacks the fire of the Holy Ghost. People will become content with just having a religious atmosphere. It's the fire of God and the heat of His Spirit that cause the snakes and vipers in people's lives to come out (Acts 28:3), and it is that same fire and heat that keep them out. The spirit of vain repetition is the one telling sign or effect of a religious atmosphere. Everything becomes a form, a ritual, and a tradition. We begin to attend meetings and services out of habit instead of in the expectancy of God's presence. People go through the outward motions of Christianity without any spiritual hunger or thirst in their hearts. The praise, worship, and music become more like entertainment than real worship. There's a knowledge of God without the intimacy of Christ or the inner working of the Holy Spirit. Knowledge without intimacy will never produce true holiness in people, but it will almost always produce pride. People are most vulnerable to deception when in this state. This is probably what happened to most of the seven churches spoken of in Revelation chapters 2 and 3. Jesus commanded some of these churches to repent. What about the leaders of these churches? Ultimately, they were to blame.

Know the Truth

Spiritual leaders are like spiritual doctors who carry a great deal of responsibility for their patients. We must be accurate in our diagnosis of them so that we can dictate the correct prescription. If our diagnosis is not accurate, then our prescription for recovery and restoration will not be accurate either. As a result, the condition of the patients will be further complicated. Leaders must develop an ability to place their finger on the pulse of God's heart and know what the Holy Ghost is saying to the Church.

We are living in the great age of information. Gaining information and knowledge is viewed as necessary for one's success. In the Church the same is true. The Bible differentiates, however, between mere knowledge and a knowledge of the truth. It says that knowledge puffs up (1 Cor. 8:1), but a knowledge of the truth will set you free (Jn. 8:32). It is easy to compromise truth for knowledge by excluding love from the equation. Love is the truth that edifies. We can be right in knowledge and wrong in love, or we can be wrong in knowledge and right in love. When knowledge of the Word of God leads us to worship our own personal success at the expense of Jesus Christ, we have departed from the truth and are walking in deception. We then become a people "ever learning, and never able to come to the knowledge of the truth" (2 Tim. 3:7 KJV). This has happened in many churches. I believe that this was the problem in the Laodicean church as well (see Rev. 3:14-22).

A form of godliness will set in when there's no zeal for God and for lost souls in a church or ministry. The earthly pursuit of success will become our goal. The Laodiceans said, "We are rich and increased with goods. We have need of nothing..." (see Rev. 3:17 KJV), but Jesus told them otherwise. Knowledge puffed them up and opened them to deception. When used wrongly, knowledge can be deadly. It can lead to the worship of humanistic ideologies and philosophies that sound like the gospel, but are not. It can also lead to the worship of success.

We have a tremendous amount of knowledge and information available to us today both naturally and spiritually. An abundance of revelation has unfolded in this generation; many voices are bidding for our attention. As a result, it is easy for leaders to become diverted from true fellowship with God and fail to hear what the Holy Ghost is saying. With the massive increase of knowledge, it is becoming easier and easier to operate out of our souls instead of our spirits. Never has it been so critical and so important to spend time alone with God. The soul will only produce the artificial and the superficial, but the Spirit will birth that which is supernatural. That's why the early apostles wanted to give themselves continually to prayer and the Word. They wanted to make sure they were giving birth to the spiritual only, to that which God wanted.

Intimacy With God

One distinct characteristic of this Church age, and a third feature of a soulish church, is the emphasis placed on doing the work of God over being in fellowship with Him, *doing* over *being*. There's an enormous rush of activity in Christians' lives today that was missing from the lives of believers in the early Church. Yet back then, spiritual results were produced almost effortlessly. The Lord added new souls to the Church daily (Acts 2:47). Now it seems a great blessing just to have annual increase. Today, few spiritual results are often produced, even with great effort on our part. We will only do what God had called us to do when we are being whom God has called us to be. The *being* must come before the *doing*. The church at Ephesus was busy *doing* without *being*. They were active, but Jesus said that they had left their first love (Rev. 2:4). He said that they could do the "first works" after returning to their first love (Rev. 2:5). The first works are those birthed from our first love, Jesus. Our part is to focus first on being a lover of Jesus Christ and a possessor of His holy nature, then spiritual reproduction will be imminent. God will have His way.

When we are truly loving Jesus, our works will be alive, not dead. The grace of God will be activated, and our works will be motivated by love. We will no longer be powerless to produce spiritual results because we will have ceased from our own works. The reason we have the *Acts* of the Apostles is because of the great power and great grace that were upon them (Acts 4:33). And such power and grace were upon them because of their great love for Jesus and for each other (Acts 4:32). The power to "be" released in them the power to "do."

There are three basic purposes to a life of prayer and fellowship with God. The first purpose of prayer is to simply *worship God*, not with the intent to receive, but to give to

God. If we do not have worship as our foundation, our prayer lives can quickly become soulish. We fellowship with God for who He is and not for what He can give us. When our lives truly become one continuous act and flow of worship, then the grace of God also flows as a continual fountain in our lives. We will have grace to be who God has called us to be and grace to do what God has called us to do. True worship is not just singing and blessing the Lord. It's a laying down of our lives on a daily basis (Rom. 12:1-2). So much of what we call prayer is governed and ruled by soulish inclinations because we don't have worship as its foundation. We've never learned to go beyond the veil and into the throne room of God. This is the only place where true intimacy happens, and it is where true spiritual vision is conceived. Once we learn to get into the Spirit in prayer, it will take less and less time to get there. We'll continually gain places in the Spirit until we finally learn to abide in fellowship with God. The next two purposes of prayer come as a result of true worship.

The second purpose of prayer is to *effect change in people and the spiritual environment of our churches, cities, and nations.* Paul prayed for the saints in the Church to grow and develop spiritually (Eph. 3:14-21). He encouraged the Church to pray for the Word to have free course in order to effect change in different places (2 Thess. 3:1 KJV). He encouraged Timothy and the Church to pray for those in authority so that a right spiritual climate could be obtained or maintained for the gospel to be spread (1 Tim. 2:1-2). At times we are to pray for political change, economic change, and social change. However, the root of all change is spiritual. Even when we pray for ourselves and our families, it is often for change in some area or situation.

The third purpose of prayer is to *receive guidance, direction, and revelation concerning the will of God*. We commune with God to be able to hear what He is saying to us. True communication with God is a dialogue. We speak to Him, but He also speaks to us.

This is all very important as it relates to spiritual vision. We are not talking about formulas, but spiritual life. As we have already stated, Laodicea was a church that opened itself up to great deception. The leadership was to blame. But take notice that it was a lack of worship and communion with the Lord that was at the center of this church's problems (Rev. 3:20). I believe that if the leaders of this Laodicean church had been "supping" with the Lord there would have been no deception.

Earlier we mentioned impatience as being one of the chief ingredients of soulish vision. Impatience conceives and then gives birth to our Ishmaels. Patience comes by being strengthened with might in the inner man (Col. 1:11), which is a direct by-product of our fellowship with God and the testing of our faith (Jas. 1:3). Fellowship with God and tests and trials strengthen our inner man. This produces patience, which then also gives birth to true spiritual vision. It's a cycle of the Spirit. Let's endeavor to be a part of that cycle.

Get in the cycle now and you will avoid being "recycled" later.

Chapter 13

Patience

Patience is a strength in our spirits that keeps us operating in the Spirit instead of out of our souls. Being patient is not the same as being slow; it is simply being in step with the timing and seasons of God. It means to move when God moves and to stop and wait when God is not moving.

The Word of God associates hastiness and impatience with foolishness.

...he that is hasty of spirit exalteth folly (Proverbs 14:29 KJV).

Do you see a man hasty in his words? There is more hope for a fool than for him (Proverbs 29:20).

The Word of God exalts the patient in spirit.

The patient in spirit in better than the proud in spirit (Ecclesiastes 7:8b).

Performance and Patience

In our fast-moving world today, it is a great challenge to possess our souls in patience. This is especially true in America. Recently, while in a conversation with a Polish immigrant, I asked him what he thought of America. His answer was very insightful and gave me a greater understanding into why our country has such an impatient soul. After I had asked this man this question, he pointed to another man walking in the near distance and said something to this effect: "Do you see that man? In my country when someone talks to him they want to know about who he is personally and about his family. In America, when someone talks to him, what they want to really know is how much money he is worth." I reflected on this man's discerning view of America, and how it spoke volumes about our culture and our churches.

The nation of America is economically based. Success is measured by a person's performance and productivity. Everything in America is fast-moving and fast-paced. Nearly everyone is "on the go." Everyone is out to perform and produce. This type of environment begins to breed tremendous impatience and restlessness in its people. Combine this with the easy access we have to almost any service or product we want (fast food, drive-through banks, credit cards, fast communications, etc.), and a culture is formed that finds it difficult to wait for anything. Time is money, so if you want more money you must make more time. We despise delays and inconveniences.

The American culture has cultivated a mindset in the soul of this nation that has a tendency to measure everything by activity and performance. Many of our churches and ministries are the same way. Results are equated with buildings and numbers. Ministries are counted as great based upon the size of their mailing list or how many countries they've visited. We have been subtly and deceptively taught to respond to appearance and hype. Because of professionalism, high technology, and an abundance of resources, appearance has become exalted over substance. It is easy to make everything look appealing and attractive. There is nothing at all wrong with having things look attractive. We should honor the Lord in appearance as well, but that is not how we are to measure spiritual success. The internal quality and spirit of a ministry should be its gauge for success, not its outward activity and appearance. In our American culture we have experts who specialize in making products and services appear to be what they are really not. Making things appear to be what they are really not has released a deceptive veil over our entire culture. False knowledge produces false success. Thus, in the church and in ministry, it becomes easy to substitute the superficial for the supernatural, the soulish for the spiritual. This type of mentality has been a main contributor to robbing the church of its spiritual power. In the region where we presently live, the largest and most beautiful church buildings are, for the most part, also the most spiritually dead.

Life or Death?

...I know your deeds; you have a reputation of being alive, but you are dead. Wake up! (Revelation 3:1-2a NIV).

This church at Sardis had a *name* and a *reputation* for being alive. In other words, to the public eye, and especially to those within the Body of Christ, this church was respected and regarded as a spiritually alive church. However, Jesus told them that there were only a few in the entire city who were undefiled (Rev. 3:4). Jesus' diagnosis of this sick church was much different than man's. Man called this church a healthy church, a spiritually alive church, but Jesus saw it differently. God does not see as man sees (1 Sam. 16:7). We need spiritual discernment to distinguish the authentic from the imitation. This particular church produced works (Rev. 3:1-2), works that Jesus said were not found perfect, for they were works that *imitated* life, but produced death. Here is where all these pieces tie together. Here is where you can fully realize how the force of patience and of waiting on God can revolutionize your life and ministry. It can cancel death and begin to produce life and power. If the soul is not trained to wait, it will imitate in order to produce. It will attempt to produce spiritual results in its own strength. This has been the curse of the Church for nearly 2,000 years. We have not learned the art of patient waiting—waiting on God.

Being active is not the equivalent of being productive, especially when it comes to the things of the Spirit. Active works can also be "dead" works. What was the prescription Jesus administered to this church in Sardis? He commanded them to repent and to watch (Rev. 2–3). He told them to hold fast to that which they had received and heard.

Pressure to perform and produce pulls many believers and ministers out of the plan and timing of God. We may even have God's plan, but reacting to pressure from either people or circumstances can pull us out of God's timing. Poor timing aborts God's plan. Pressure to perform and produce can lead you into a life and ministry that is cut off from God's grace.

When Lazarus was sick and his sisters sent for Jesus, He did not panic and rush to his side. Instead, He waited. His spirit had not alerted Him to go right away. Yet Jesus knew that He was to go and raise Lazarus up (Jn. 11:1-6). Jesus had the plan, and He stayed in the Spirit despite outside pressure. It's important not only to know the "what" but also the "when" of God's plan. Jesus walked in patience, and He knew that He could do nothing without the unction of the Father (Jn. 5:19,30). He imitated only what He saw the Father doing and what He heard the Father saying. That's how the Church is built. That is spiritual vision. When we stop depending on God and the leading of His Spirit we become imitators of men. We begin to rely on the wisdom of men or on past plans, strategies, and instructions. What happens to many of us is that we try and duplicate what happened in the Spirit before or what we've been taught by the precepts of men. We like easy formulas or how-to steps because we do not like to patiently wait on God.

Power in Patience

The early Church began by waiting on God (Acts 1:4). Waiting on God empowered them for service. Waiting on God released the Holy Spirit's power to perform signs and wonders in the fullness of time. It arrested people's attention and caused them to be amazed and to marvel (Acts 2:7). Waiting on God, not just once, but continually, produced the power of God throughout the Book of Acts. Living works of God were demonstrated through living vessels of God. It brought Ananias to minister to Saul (Acts 9:10-18), and it released the word of the Lord to him. Think about the implications of this one incredible act of obedience that came as a result of waiting on God. Waiting on God brought Peter to the house of Cornelius to preach, thereby opening the door to the entire Gentile world (Acts 10). Again, this all came from one simple act of obedience to the word of the Lord from both Peter and Cornelius.

Waiting on God separated Paul and Barnabas to the ministry of apostleship (Acts 13:1-4), a critical transition in their ministry that eventually produced a great expansion of the Kingdom of God.

One of the greatest examples of patience in a time of great conflict and pressure was displayed by King David. Now, remember, David was a man whose soul had been harnessed and trained. He learned patience through serving under Saul's leadership. The severe trials brought upon David through Saul's wickedness worked great patience into David during his early years. In First Samuel 30, we see him facing what may have been his most severe trial. Let's see how he handled it.

When David and his men arrived home from battle to the city of Ziklag, they found it burned and their wives and children taken captive. David and his men wept until they had no more strength to weep. David was very distressed, not only because of the destruction of the city and the kidnapping of all the families, but because his own men began to speak of stoning him due to their indescribable grief. Notice what David did.

> *...But David strengthened himself in the Lord his God. Then David said to Abiathar the priest, Ahimelech's son, "Please bring the ephod here to me." And Abiathar brought the ephod to David. So David inquired at the Lord, saying, "Shall I pursue this troop? Shall I overtake them?" And He answered him, "Pursue, for you shall surely overtake them and without fail recover all"* (1 Samuel 30:6-8).

Even under very extreme pressure, David would not move until he heard from God. David was a man after

God's own heart. He had been broken of self-confidence
and pride. He had learned not to move with any sort of plan
without God's leading. Let's look at another instance where
he refused to move without inquiring of the Lord.

After the Philistines heard that David had been anointed
king they set out to search for him, but David heard about it
and went out to confront them. But before he did, he again
inquired of the Lord.

> *And David inquired of God, saying, "Shall I go up
> against the Philistines? Will You deliver them into my
> hand?" And the Lord said to him, "Go up, for I will
> deliver them into your hand"* (1 Chronicles 14:10).

Notice God's response to David's request and the ensuing results (1 Chron. 14:11-12). It happened just as the Lord
had said. But the Philistines wouldn't quit, so they offered a
counterattack. Now instead of growing self-confident and
depending on his first victory, notice David's heart attitude
and spiritual posture: He returned to seek the Lord again.

> *Therefore David inquired again of God, and God
> said to him, "You shall not go up after them; circle
> around them, and come upon them in front of the
> mulberry trees"* (1 Chronicles 14:14).

This time, the Lord gave David a whole new strategy
and set of instructions. As at the first, God wrought a great
victory for David and his men. David could have easily as-
sumed another victory without consulting God again. He
could have grown confident in his own ability to handle the
situation. After all, David and his men were skilled war-
riors, but David had learned to wait on God.

Restlessness: The Antichrist Spirit

*But the wicked are like the troubled sea, when it can-
not rest, whose waters cast up mire and dirt* (Isaiah
57:20).

The wicked cannot rest. The wicked one is the antichrist
(2 Thess. 2:8 KJV). Antichrist means anti-anointing, for
Christ means the Messiah, the Anointed One. A spirit of
restlessness and impatience is anti-anointing. It is contrary
to the anointing of God (1 Jn. 2:18-19).

We have an unction from the Holy One (1 Jn. 2:20 KJV).
We are not antichrist. This unction or anointing is what
teaches us and causes us to abide in Him (1 Jn. 2:27).
Follow the unction. Follow the anointing. Wait patiently for
it. Don't do anything without it. Don't move without it, or
you'll birth an Ishmael. Imitate what you hear and see from
the Holy One. If He's not speaking or showing you anything, then keep doing what you're doing.

When I graduated from Bible school, many of my
friends went out into their own ministries. Some started
churches, and others began traveling or going to the mission
field. Some encouraged me to step out in faith and go
preach as well. The voices of men were telling me to get out
of my so-called comfort zone. I kept seeking the Lord about
it and had no release in my spirit to do anything but what I
had already been doing, which was being faithful at my
local church. I knew that God had called me to preach, and
I knew the time would come soon. However, soon does not
mean now. I waited and went in God's timing instead. I cast
off impatience and clothed myself with patience. Others
went before their time, and some of them are not even in
ministry today. They aborted God's plan for their lives by

not completing the process of preparation God had for them. If we are going to be vessels fit for the Master's use, we must first purge ourselves from the precepts of men and learn the ways of the Spirit of God.

When it seems to you as if time has become slow or delayed, remember patience. When circumstances and situations are sending your mind into an emotional frenzy, remember patience. When tests and trials press upon you, remember patience. During apparent failure or defeat, remember patience. When chaos causes people to react and panic, remember patience. Under the heat and pressure of life, remember patience.

For when your patience is finally in full bloom, then you will be ready for anything, strong in character, full and complete (James 1:4b TLB).

Your patience will bloom like a flower.
You'll be in step and in season with every hour.
Perfect peace will rain on you as a shower.
And you'll be filled continually with God's power
As you wait on the Lord.

Chapter 14

Trusting the Holy Spirit

The general populace did not think they were ready. "They're too young and inexperienced," they said. "The work will suffer, and the ministry will not last." But we knew that it was time to let go and turn the mission over to national leadership.

Relinquishing Control

During our years of serving the Lord in West Africa, whenever our missionary team would enter into a new city and nation, it was always with the thought of working ourselves out of a job. In the last country we lived in, most of the ministry leadership was provided by myself, my wife, and another missionary couple. At the same time that the Lord released us to turn the work over and return to the States, the other couple received instructions from the Lord to open a new work in another African country. From a natural standpoint, it seemed premature for all four of us to leave; but the Spirit of God had bore witness with all of us that it was time.

Emotionally, it's always difficult to let your natural children go, especially when it's time for them to leave home. They've been under your protection and leadership all their lives. You've always provided for them. When they finally leave, it can be a heart-wrenching experience for parents. Spiritually, it is the same way. When your emotions and your soul want to hold onto your spiritual children, you must still let go. If you don't, then you will stifle the work that God wants to do in them. In each of these countries, it has been our testimony that whenever we let go, the influence of the Holy Spirit gave greater increase than if we had remained in authority.

> *But I tell you the truth, it is to your advantage that I go away; for if I do not go away, the Helper* [Holy Spirit] *shall not come to you...* (John 16:7 NAS).

> *So when they had appointed elders in every church, and prayed with fasting, they commended them to the Lord in whom they had believed* (Acts 14:23).

Jesus and the early apostles did not have any problem relinquishing control. They trusted the Holy Spirit to supply the grace and sufficiency to the disciples they had taught and trained. When any leader begins to believe that he is indispensable and that others really cannot function without him, God will eventually remove His grace from him. There are three basic elements that we must give to people who have proven to be disciples of Jesus Christ. They are *training*, *authority*, and *liberty*. If we only give them one or two of these, they will be lacking. If we give them training and authority, but no liberty, they will be oppressed. It is a bondage to be trusted with a position of authority, and yet have little liberty to make decisions. Is it possible to have authority without liberty? It is if every time a subordinate makes decisions the leader is looking over his shoulder. We need to trust the Holy Spirit, but we also need to trust the men whom we have discipled. If we only give them training and liberty but no authority, they will be frustrated. If we give them liberty and authority, but no training, they will be unskilled at what they do.

Releasing Responsibly

After being adequately trained and proven, disciples need to be released. Every decision they make thereafter should not have to be funneled through the leader. We're not saying there shouldn't continue to be some oversight and accountability, especially if the disciple is under the leader's authority, but at that point, more trust should be placed on the Holy Spirit than the leader. In John 16:7, Jesus said in so many words, "If I don't leave or let go, the Holy Spirit won't come." I have found that if the relationship is healthy between the leader and the disciple, it's usually the disciple who doesn't want himself or the leader to part. Conversely, if the relationship is governed by control and oppression, the disciple finds great relief when out from under the constant supervision of the leader.

Our focus for this chapter is to impart a greater ability for leaders to entrust the Holy Spirit with men and women they've trained. What this adds up to is less control and more mobility. If people have been taught and trained correctly and have proven themselves faithful, greater mobility will always mean a greater increase to the Kingdom of God. The church is local, but it is also mobile. The building where the church meets may be stationary, but the people are to be mobile. It is leadership's responsibility to mobilize them. Many churches never grow because there's no free flow. We want the people to be moving parts in the Body of Christ. It's the oil of the Holy Ghost that generates both mobility and fluidity in the Church and causes every member to be a moving part. Give the Spirit more place, and He will create more space for all the moving parts. Disciples will flow freely in an oily atmosphere, and leaders will find that the entire church engine will function at a much greater capacity. Leadership's biggest responsibility is to periodically give the engine an oil change. Keeping the oil fresh will allow the engine to stay mobile, fluid, and clean. When leadership is anointed with the oil of the Holy Ghost, it is difficult to rub them the wrong way. The people will then be liberated (lubricated), not bound.

Allow me to give warning to one type of leader. If you are a super-organized person and have a perfectionist spirit, beware. Carnal perfectionism and organization suffocates the Holy Spirit. What we are after is the order of the Spirit, not the order of man. Where there is mobility and fluidity, excessive movement will create the appearance of disorder. We are not promising a trouble-free movement of the Holy Spirit and of people. There will be accidents and mishaps. Jesus had them with His disciples, but look at the fruit. Let it go, and it will grow. Let go, and let God.

One last word of admonition: When I say to let go and let God, I am not condoning slothfulness on the leader's part. This is not an excuse for being unorganized and uninformed. What I am encouraging is for leadership to press in to the realm of the Spirit as opposed to the realm of the soul or the arm of flesh. Jesus and the early apostles didn't just commit their disciples and followers to the Lord. They prayed and fasted while they were doing it. I personally believe that Jesus always prayed for His disciples, but probably not always as much as He did toward the end of His earthly ministry. Once again, when it comes to staff personnel or people you've trained, commit them to the Lord from the beginning and trust the Holy Spirit's ministry to them. Oversee them, and help them when they need it. Encourage and motivate them, but do not control and stifle them. Your life will be much simpler, and everyone will be much happier.

Chapter 15

Despise Not Leadership

And he said to his men, "The Lord forbid that I should do this thing to my master, the Lord's anointed, to stretch out my hand against him, seeing he is the Lord's anointed" (1 Samuel 24:6).

I would do a great disservice to the Body of Christ if I failed to include this chapter in this book. This is for those few who are forever among us who will always want to take matters into their own hands. I call these "spiritual policemen"; they are always looking for any violation in leadership so they can blow their new whistles that came straight from some Cracker Jack box. To them I say, "Hold on, rebel! You are out of line!"

If the words of this book were used to incite rebellion in the Body of Christ, I would forever have remorse and regret in my heart for even writing it. Although this book is addressed to leaders, it is not limited to such. There are people who may read this book and begin to arrogantly and defiantly oppose their leaders and pastors if it was not for this short chapter. If you are contemplating bringing correction to your leader or pastor as a result of having read this book, think again.

God Never Honors Rebellion

First of all, it is not the place of children to correct their parents. The Word clearly states that you are not to rebuke an elder (1 Tim. 5:1). You have no scriptural grounds to do so. The only way even an associate minister has authority to correct a head minister is if he is given permission to do so. You have no authority to correct leadership unless they've given you that authority. Correction comes out of proper relationship and covenant. The only one who has a right to bring correction to a minister of the gospel besides his or her own spouse is usually another minister. Let me ask you something. When did David ever correct Saul? When did Samuel ever correct Eli? Some people sincerely believe that their leader is wicked. However, there are not too many men more wicked than Saul or more irresponsible than Eli. These men were two of the poorest examples of leadership in the Bible, and yet neither David nor Samuel, who were under their leadership, ever retaliated against them. It is only a testimony to one's own ignorance if one attempts to do what these two anointed young men of God refused to do. When correction is brought from a younger to an elder or from outside the sphere of covenant relationship, it is what I call soulish correction. It is done out of the soul and not the spirit.

"But," you say, "what if I'm right?" Even if your allegations against your leader or pastor are true, you are still wrong in principle and in violation of the Scriptures. Two wrongs never make a right. Study David's life and his submission to Saul. Who was wrong? Who was evil? Who had a bad spirit and wrong motives? Without question, it was Saul. Still, it was never right for David to retaliate. Look at the life and ministry of Jesus. Study Him as He stood on trial before Pilate. Who was right and who was wrong? Was there ever a more innocent man than our Lord Jesus Christ? Yet He remained speechless against Pilate and the accusations of the people. He refused to even defend Himself. Instead, Jesus committed Himself to God, who judges righteously (1 Pet. 2:23). If He had retaliated and dishonored authority, Jesus would have been committing Himself to be judged by man.

Let me explain further. There are spiritual laws and principles in the Word of God. When two spiritual laws seem to conflict, you should always yield to the higher law. For instance, gravity is a law. It tells us that if we leap or fall off a high building, we will descend. However, there is a higher law than gravity. It is the law of aerodynamics, or "lift and thrust," which enables an aircraft to get off the ground and stay in the sky. The spiritual principles of authority and submission also are higher laws. Error in authority gives us no right to rebuke or rebel against that authority.

Allow me to give you another example from the Scriptures. Contrary to the law, the high priest ordered Paul to be smitten on the mouth, but Paul was acting contrary to the law as well when he spoke against the high priest (Acts 23:1-5). Once again, two wrongs do not make a right. There is a higher law at work. The spiritual law of honoring authority remains a higher law, whether he's right or wrong. God's Word commands us to not only submit to the good but to the froward and evil as well (1 Pet. 2:18 KJV).

What if the leader is involved in unscriptural practices or tells you to do something that's completely unscriptural? What if your leader is just way off base? Then you must submit to your conscience and to God without any outward rebellion and dishonor to your leader. This is where people miss it many times. They rebel and dishonor the leader outwardly and leave the church or ministry. Then they go out and constantly speak against him. Now I'm not saying that you shouldn't leave, but, as bad as it may seem, I would not have anyone leave unless the Lord told that person to leave. You see, sometimes the Lord will use wicked and corrupt leadership to test you and to work great character in you that otherwise wouldn't be produced any other way. (I know this is not what you wanted to hear or read, but nevertheless, it's the truth.)

A Righteous Response to Leadership

What should you do if you find yourself under corrupt leadership? First of all, *corrupt* is a pretty strong word. What I find in most cases is that a person's leader is never as bad as he or she has been described. Your view of them may be based on a misconception that you have or even a biased interpretation of what you believe poor leadership to be. You may have to look in the mirror of your own heart and provide an honest examination of your own attitude. Do you truly believe that you are under a "Saul" or an "Eli"? If not, then the testimony of the Scriptures advise you to stick to your leader and stay right where you are. Let God develop some real character and backbone in you by honoring and submitting to leadership, even when it's difficult. Now, if you're not being fed the Word of God and having your spiritual needs met, that's an entirely different story. Leave right now. Go find green pastures, and don't ever look back. However, most people are just looking for any excuse they can find to oppose leadership. Many will leave good churches and ministries simply because they were hurt or offended by something that was either said or done to them. Many times it wasn't even the leadership that offended them. If after thorough and honest examination you are still convinced that you are under some pretty "bad" leadership, do what David and Samuel did:

1. Leave only if the Lord absolutely leads you. Otherwise, stay.

2. Pray for your leader.

3. Forgive your leader.

4. Minister to the Lord.

5. Do not rejoice if your leader falls or is judged by the Lord.

6. Repent if you've fallen short somewhere in the above list.

Praying, forgiving, and ministering to the Lord will keep your spirit joyful, strong, and free, even under the most adverse circumstances. This is what David and Samuel did. Not only that, but both David and Samuel grieved over Saul's death. They did not rejoice. They did not have the attitude of, "Well, that serves him right. He got what he deserved." No, they mourned. God Himself judged Saul, but even in that judgment, David and Samuel would not rejoice. Oh, for such a true and loyal heart as these two men possessed!

Many people miss God in this area. They base everything on their feelings and emotions, and on the mere happenstance of being "right." Eventually, if these people don't get their hearts right, they wind up on the spiritual junk heap of life, castaways.

In closing this chapter, let me illustrate something. You may drive your automobile up to an intersection. If the light is red, you must brake and wait. Once the light turns green, you have the right of way. But, wait a second. If in the corner of your eye, you spot another vehicle speeding toward the intersection from the right, what will you do? It looks like the driver of this high speed vehicle either doesn't see the red light or he just doesn't care. At any rate, if based on having the right of way and a green light, you decide to proceed through the intersection, the high-speed vehicle may suddenly swerve and brake and try to avoid hitting your vehicle. However, if he fails to maneuver out of your path and rams into you, demolishing your vehicle and killing you, who was right? You were. Who is now dead? You are. Tell me, was it worth it? When it comes to dealing with this area of leadership, you can be right, but you can also be "dead" right.

With your pastor or leader, don't ever be caught "dead" right.

Chapter 16

Is Jesus Enough for You?

Ishmael was a product of Abraham's soul. He was born outside of God's time and purpose. He was ordered cast out. An Ishmael is anything that we birth outside of God's will and purpose for our lives. An Ishmael is the futile efforts of man to manifest a promise of God.

An Ishmael may represent the strong soul ties that believers have with anything or anyone in their lives that stands in the way of the perfect will of God for them. Ishmael will comfort and accommodate our souls at the expense of our spirits. Ishmaels may bring us pleasure for a season, but in the end, they will mock us and render us ineffective to produce spiritual results.

The more we hold onto an Ishmael, the more grievous it will become for us to cast him out. We do not lay our Ishmaels on the altar, but we cast them out of our lives. The casting out of our Ishmaels is not a service we do for God, but for ourselves.

Here is what an Ishmael is like. While out shopping one day, a little boy may spot a toy that he really wants and asks his daddy to purchase it for him. His daddy may promise to buy the toy in due season. Time passes, and although the child has his daddy's promise, the manifestation of it is too slow for him. He grows impatient and begins to reason and devise a faster way to obtain the promised toy. So, he finds another adult to go and purchase the toy for him. The little boy loves the toy and spends a great deal of time with it. However, his daddy is grieved because of his son's lack of patience and trust in his promise. This is the same process by which Ishmaels are often born. Ishmael is something we birth as a result of a promise of God.

Isaac was different. To Abraham, Isaac was a fulfilled promise of God. He was born of God's perfect will and purpose. He was born in God's perfect way and in God's perfect time. In the lives of believers, Isaac is symbolic of everything that is pure and right. He is God's vision for our lives. He represents that which is spiritual, but God demands him as a sacrificial offering. Our Isaacs cannot take the place of God. It is our Isaacs that God calls us to lay on the altar. This is the holy and the acceptable sacrifice that is pleasing to God.

Here is what an Isaac can be like. An Isaac can be like that same father who purchases a toy for his little son. He does so out of a love for him and wants to share in the joy of what his labor has purchased. However, if the son begins to devote all his time, energy, and attention to the toy at the neglect of spending time with his father, then the father will become saddened, hurt, and grieved. This is what believers can do with the blessings of God in their lives. This is what leaders and ministers can do with their spiritual gifts, vision, and goals. We can become busy going somewhere, doing something, and trying to be somebody at the expense of God's heart.

Just like a child who asks his daddy to fix the toy when it breaks, or to buy him a bigger and better toy, so leaders often petition God with regard to their lives and ministries. We ask the Lord to help us build our ministry. We ask Him to help us promote the vision and raise funds and resources for it. We tack God onto our lives and ministries so that He can help us improve them. Our ministries then become our idols. We study the Bible to get another good message to promote our ministry. We pray to get more power and anointing to promote our ministry. Then if we're not careful, we begin to add our own plans to God's plan and then ask Him to bless them. This can be compared to the love for the toy growing in the child's heart while his daddy stands by waiting for the day when that love will turn back to him.

Dear children, keep away from anything that might take God's place in your hearts. Amen (1 John 5:21 TLB).

Is Jesus enough for you? One day I heard this question rise up in my spirit. It was posed to me during a time of transition for our family as we were launching a new ministry. This question was asked me during a season when God was imparting fresh vision and fresh opportunities for ministry into our lives. God gave us His plan. It was birthed by His Spirit. It was an Isaac. But, we still needed to stop and consider the question. If, however, we didn't have a ministry, a vision, and so many new opportunities, would we be satisfied with just Jesus?

You see, if there are any idols in our lives, then Jesus is not enough. It is not wrong to have things. It's certainly not wrong to have a ministry and a vision that the Lord Himself has entrusted you with. But if they ever take the place of

Jesus, then they are wrong. Jesus will not share you with other lovers. He wants you for Himself. He doesn't want to just occupy a part of our lives; He wants all of our lives.

Is Jesus enough for you? Don't be too quick to answer this question. Ponder it, and let it do a deep work in your heart. May the solemnity of this question cause reflection and great searching of heart in our lives until we become totally stripped of all selfish ambition and false motives. Let us truly allow the Lord Jesus to reign supreme over our lives and any ministry that He has entrusted to us.

Chapter 17

Prophetic Utterance: Restoration of the Body of Christ

Mending and restoration of the Body is at the head of God's current agenda. God wants everyone in their place, whole and functioning according to His purpose. God's glory shall fill His temple and cover the earth as His people find and renew their function in the Body. Many believers are hurt, distraught, brokenhearted, and confused. Just as parts of our physical body become hurt and do not function properly (or at all), so there are those in Christ's Body who are in need of healing. The Lord loves His Body and wants to restore all to His glory.

For no one ever hated his own flesh, but nourishes and cherishes it, just as the Lord does the church (Ephesians 5:29).

Leaders of some ministries are partly responsible for the fall of their subordinates because of their lack of love, integrity, and obedience. This is why God is now making a clear call to leaders to bring healing and restoration to His Body:

"Be sensitive to My Body and to My people. Be careful to be a voice for unity and not division, edification and not destruction. Be a voice for love and not jealousy and envy which is born of hate and is sensual and devilish."

Today, portions of the Body are malfunctioning or not functioning at all. They may be in the wrong place, with the wrong people and the wrong plan or vision for their lives. These persons establish the will of God only with their natural minds and thereby retard God's plan and purpose for their lives. They are floundering here and there, outside of their rightful place in the Body. In some places, we have a hand trying to be a foot, an eye trying to be an ear, or a mouth trying to be a nose. As a result, we have a dysfunctional Body. Still others are like, as it were, an arm in a cast or a paralyzed part not functioning at all.

And the Lord weeps for His Body....

For there are yet others who are fighting each other as a right hand would fight the left hand, seemingly in their rightful place, but operating with a wrong spirit, which leads to disillusionment and deception.

The Body must begin to hearken to the voice of the Lord the Shepherd, and move as one in love. When one rejoices, all should rejoice. When one suffers, all should suffer. Like when one hammers a nail and hits his thumb, the body will cringe with pain and move to the aid of that one, so should it be with the Body of Christ.

The Lord weeps for His Body....

"This is the day of mending and restoration. This is the day and this is the hour when My Body shall be filled with My glory and walk in My power. To the Light many shall come and walk therein, so that which was dysfunctional shall be functional, and that which was broken shall be mended and restored, and that which was out of place shall be put in place. And those parts which were not working shall work, and many that were sad shall be made glad and rejoice, and walk in the light and glory of God.

"And the glory of many shall be as one. And as the demons of darkness cried out when they recognized the glorious Christ, so shall My enemies recognize the glory of My Church and be scattered. My glory shall fill My temple, and My Body shall march in rank as everyone hears My voice and calling. And they shall find their place and submit to the grace which I've given unto them.

"And many of My leaders shall humble themselves and call Me Lord. And there shall be a gathering of My eagles who soar in the heavenlies and hear My voice on high. And they shall give direction to those in rank below, and there shall be a mighty and a great flow on the earth below…a flow of My direction and plan in the hearts of men, and then a flow of My glory and power as they march in rank again. It shall be as the latter house I've spoken of, full of the glory of God.

"And as an army moves according to instructions from its heads, so shall My army move. And just as there are specializations in the army of place and function, so shall there be a greater precision of these things in My army. And just as some operate in the air, on the sea, or on the land, so shall My troops find their specialty and place of operation. These are the beginning stages of new training. A new breed of leaders shall arise who are given to God and His plan. These are the days of accurate impartation and precision in spiritual training. And it shall be said of these that they march to the beat of a different spirit, and many shall recognize the hand of the Lord upon them. It shall be much different for the spirits of many shall be enlightened, and the humble shall be exalted and given more grace to function in their God-given place.

"Put on the helmet of salvation and take up the shield of faith. Let the breastplate of righteousness and the belt of truth be in its place. Let your feet be shod with the preparation of the gospel of peace, and be ready to run. Sharpen yourself with the sword of the Spirit and make way in your heart for the Lord.

"For you shall hear His voice and march to it, and others shall join in this glorious number. And war shall be in their plans, and love shall be their purpose. And the enemies who oppose them shall regret their stand, when in that day the Lord's army does march to His command. There shall be a shaking and a trembling from the noise they hear, and as the Light breaks forth they shall be filled with fear.

"The training shall commence, and for many be intense, for the work and the harvest is great, and many battles are yet to be won...and the race to be run. To all goes forth the call. To answer is their choice...To march with Me and hear My voice shall cause many to rejoice. But to be called and neglect shall bring great regret to the hearts of many. But to yield to the training, the training...Yes, there is so much training yet to be done...so much impartation to be made...And so they shall enter training camp and yield to be trained and rejoice therein."

Hallelujah! Thank You, Lord.

Ministry Information

The vision of Holy Fire Ministries is to ignite revival fires in churches, cities, and nations across the world.

For information on Holy Fire Ministries, a listing of other materials by Bert M. Farias, or information on our missionary outreaches, especially in the 10/40 window of the world, contact:

Holy Fire Ministries
P.O. Box 36368
Pensacola, FL 32516-6368

e-mail: HolyFireMin@juno.com
phone: 888-996-PURE

Internship Program

Holy Fire Ministries assists the Brownsville Revival School of Ministry in a program designed to rally young students toward the call of God. It involves training and sending them on special assignments with an emphasis on spreading the spirit of revival and helping Stateside churches with evangelistic outreach.

Apprenticeship Program

Holy Fire Ministries helps mentor young ministers who sense the call of God to leadership, especially as an evangelist or a short-term/long-term missionary. This more advanced program exists to instill confidence in these apprentices by granting them the opportunity for hands-on training.

Both of these programs presently work in conjunction with the Brownsville Revival School of Ministry. For more information on the school, please call (850) 458-6787.

Other
Destiny Image titles
you will enjoy reading

THE GOD CHASERS
by Tommy Tenney.
Are you dissatisfied with "church"? Are you looking for more? Do you yearn to touch God? You may be a *God chaser*! The passion of Tommy Tenney, evangelist and third-generation Pentecostal minister, is to "catch" God and find himself in God's manifest presence. For too long God's children have been content with crumbs. The Father is looking for those who will seek His face. This book will enflame your own desire to seek God with your whole heart and being—and to find Him.
ISBN 0-7684-2016-4 $11.99p

ENCOUNTERING THE PRESENCE
by Colin Urquhart.
What is it about Jesus that, when we encounter Him, we are changed? When we encounter the Presence, we encounter the Truth, because Jesus is the Truth. Here Colin Urquhart, best-selling author and pastor in Sussex, England, explains how the Truth changes facts. Do you desire to become more like Jesus? The Truth will set you free!
ISBN 0-7684-2018-0 $10.99p

GOD CAN USE LITTLE OLE ME
by Randy Clark.
Do you believe that God uses only the educated, the dynamic, and the strong in faith to do the work of His Kingdom? Be prepared to be surprised! In this practical, down-to-earth book, Randy Clark shows that God uses ordinary people, often in extraordinary ways, to accomplish His purposes. Through his own personal experience and the testimonies of other "little ole me's," Randy shows that God still heals today, and that He is using everyday Christians to be involved with Him in a healing ministry to the world.
ISBN 1-56043-696-4 $9.99p

Available at your local Christian bookstore.

Internet: http://www.reapernet.com

Other
Destiny Image titles
you will enjoy reading

THE COSTLY ANOINTING
by Lori Wilke.
In this book, teacher and prophetic songwriter Lori Wilke boldly reveals God's requirements for being entrusted with an awesome power and authority. She speaks directly from God's heart to your heart concerning the most costly anointing. This is a word that will change your life!
ISBN 1-56043-051-6 $9.99p

THE HIDDEN POWER OF PRAYER AND FASTING
by Mahesh Chavda.
How do you react when overwhelming defeat stares you in the eye? What do you do when faced with insurmountable odds? God has provided a way to turn certain defeat into awesome victory—through prayer and fasting! An international evangelist and the senior pastor of All Nations Church in Charlotte, North Carolina, Mahesh Chavda has seen firsthand the power of God released through a lifestyle of prayer and fasting. Here he shares from decades of personal experience and scriptural study principles and practical tips about fasting and praying. This book will inspire you to tap into God's power and change your life, your city, and your nation!
ISBN 0-7684-2017-2 $9.99p

THE LOST ART OF INTERCESSION
by Jim W. Goll.
The founder of Ministry to the Nations, Jim Goll has traveled the world in a teaching and prophetic ministry. All over the globe God is moving—He is responding to the prayers of His people. Here Jim Goll teaches the lessons learned by the Moravians during their 100-year prayer Watch. They sent up prayers; God sent down His power. Through Scripture, the Moravian example, and his own prayer life, Jim Goll proves that "what goes up must come down."
ISBN 1-56043-697-2 $9.99p

Available at your local Christian bookstore.

Internet: http://www.reapernet.com